The Piano Compendium

A Selection of Pieces for Piano

Book 3
Grades 7-8

KONSTANTINOS PAPATHEODOROU

Erebus Society

First published in Great Britain in 2018
Erebus Society

First Edition

Arrangement © Konstantinos Papatheodorou 2018
Cover © Constantin Vaughn 2018

ISBN 978-1-912461-08-0

www.erebussociety.com

TABLE OF CONTENTS

GRADE 7

Moments Musicaux
Opus 94 in F Minor

Franz Schubert

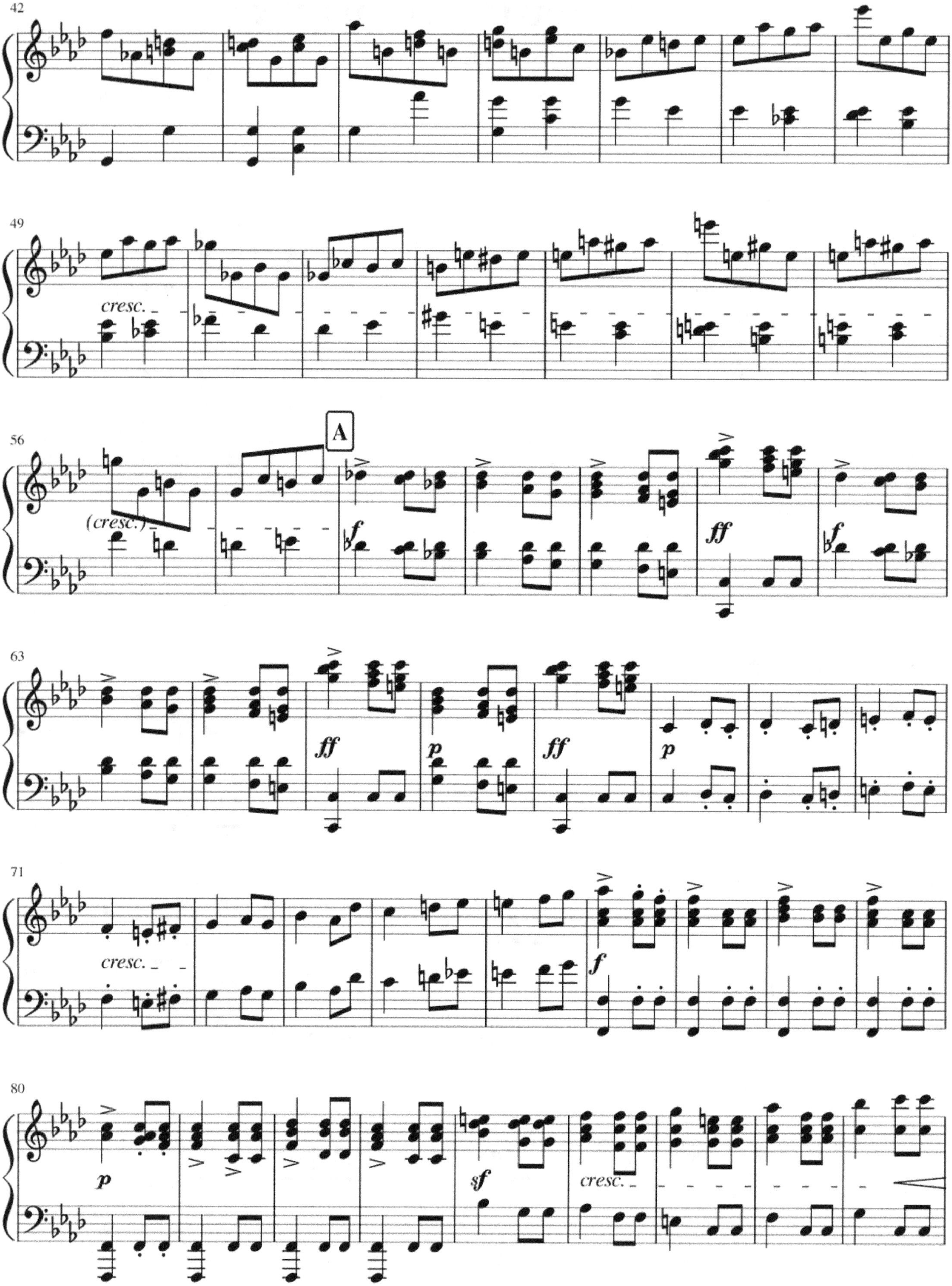
42
49
cresc.
56
(cresc.)
A
f
ff
63
p
71
cresc.
80
sf
cresc.

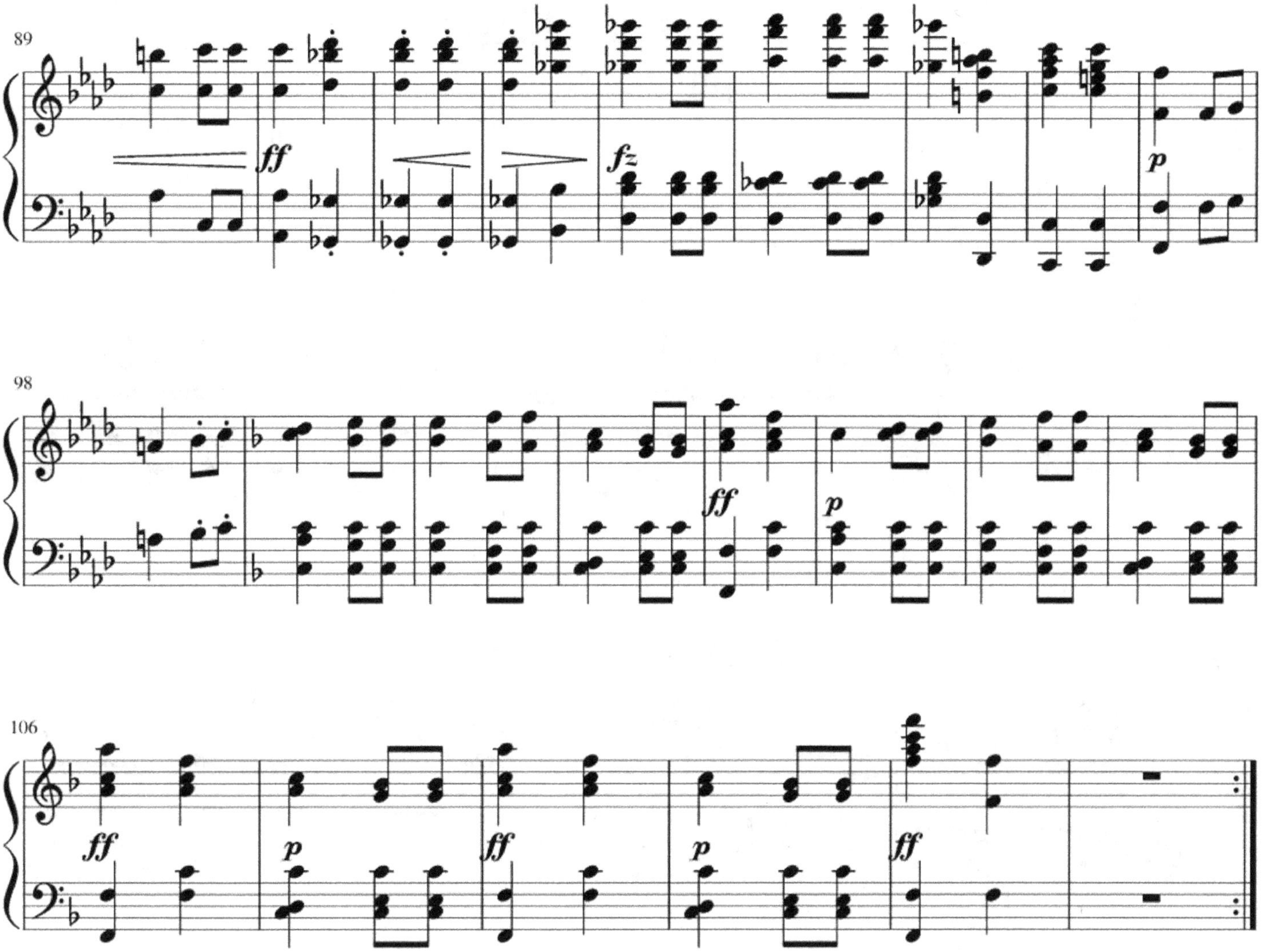

Etude in E Major
Opus 10, No 3

Frédéric François Chopin

17
a tempo
ten.
ff
ten.
sempre legato
ten.
dim.
rall.
pp
21
poco più animato
p
25
28
cresc.
f
31
p
f
p
sf
f
Ped

34
f
p
f
p
Ped
37
sf
f
p
39
sf
p
sf
p
41
8va
ff
con forza
Ped
44
8va
con forza
con bravura
f
Ped
Ped
Ped

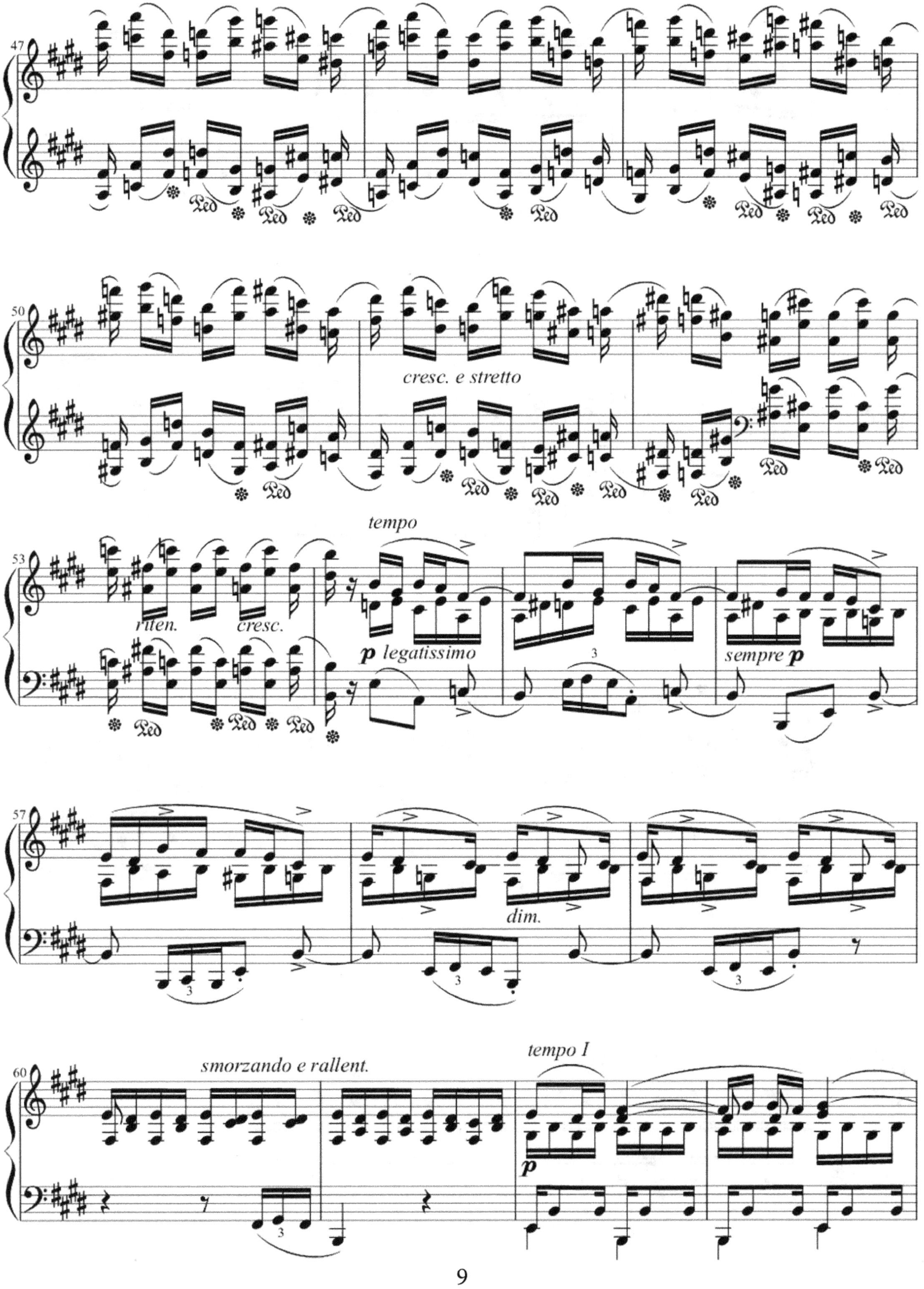
47
50
cresc. e stretto
tempo
53
riten.
cresc.
p legatissimo
sempre p
57
dim.
60
smorzando e rallent.
tempo I
p

64
poco cresc.
68
cresc. e stretto
ritenuto
cresc.
a tempo
f
71
dim.
pp
75
ritenuto
smorz.

Nocturne in C Minor
Opus 48, No 1

Frédéric François Chopin

11

ten.
cresc.
ten.
dim.
Poco più lento
sotto voce e sostenuto
sempre p
poco cresc.
dim.
pp
cresc.

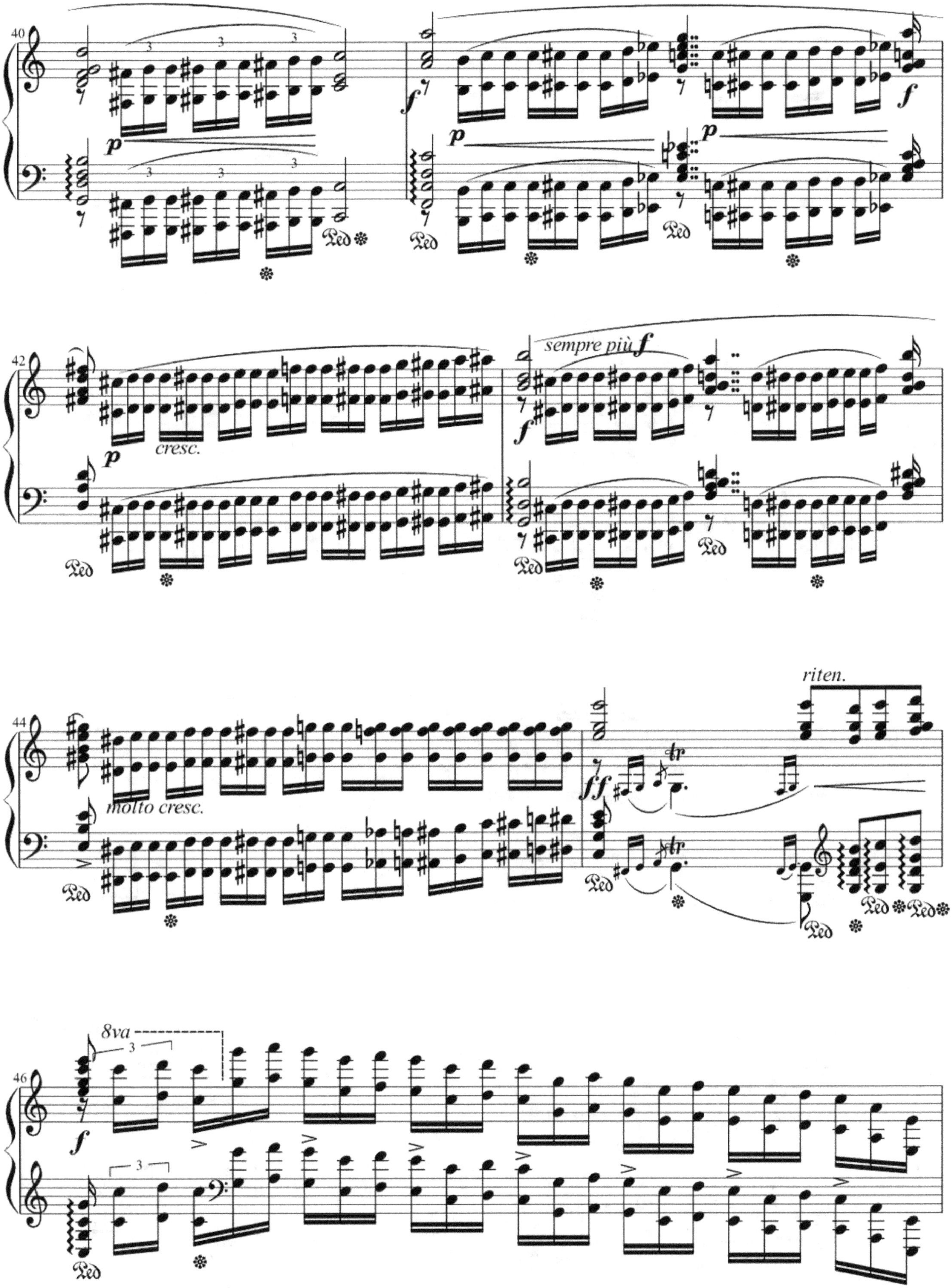
sempre più f
cresc.
molto cresc.
riten.
8va

47
sempre ff
riten.
8va
accel.
48
dim.
Doppi movimento
agitato
pp
50
52
sempre pp

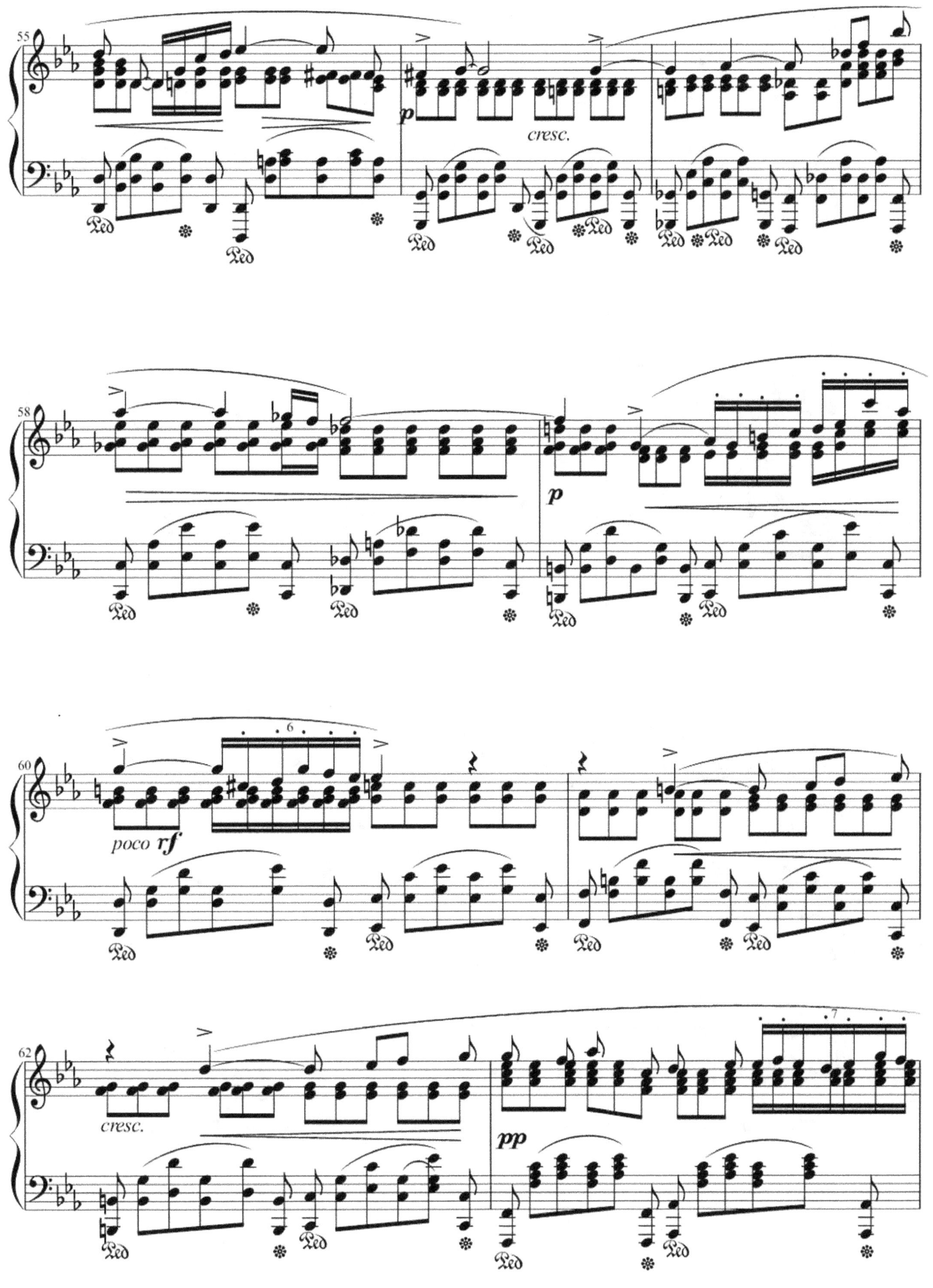
55
p
cresc.
58
p
60
poco rf
62
cresc.
pp

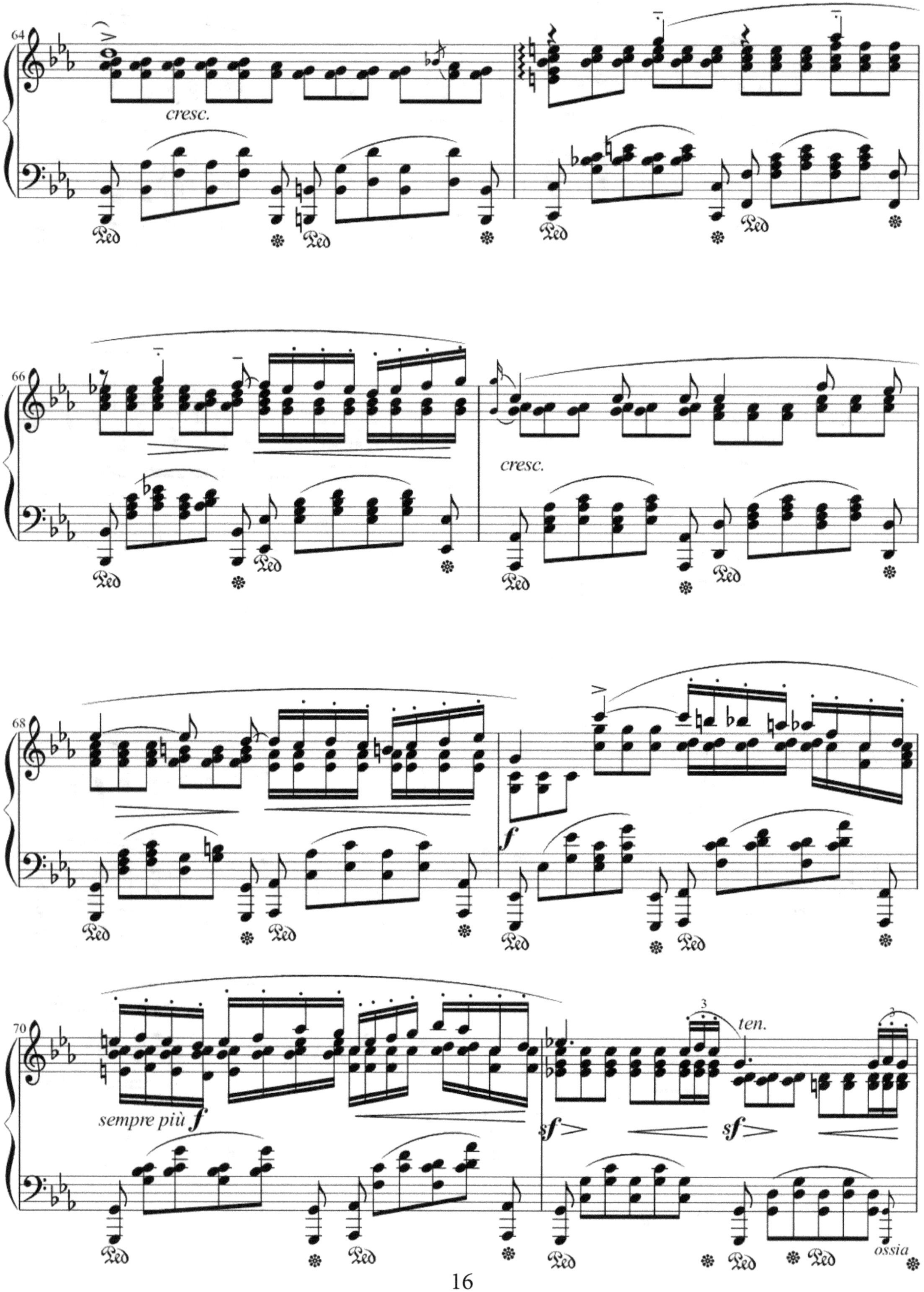
64
cresc.
66
cresc.
68
f
70
sempre più f
sf
sf
ten.
ossia

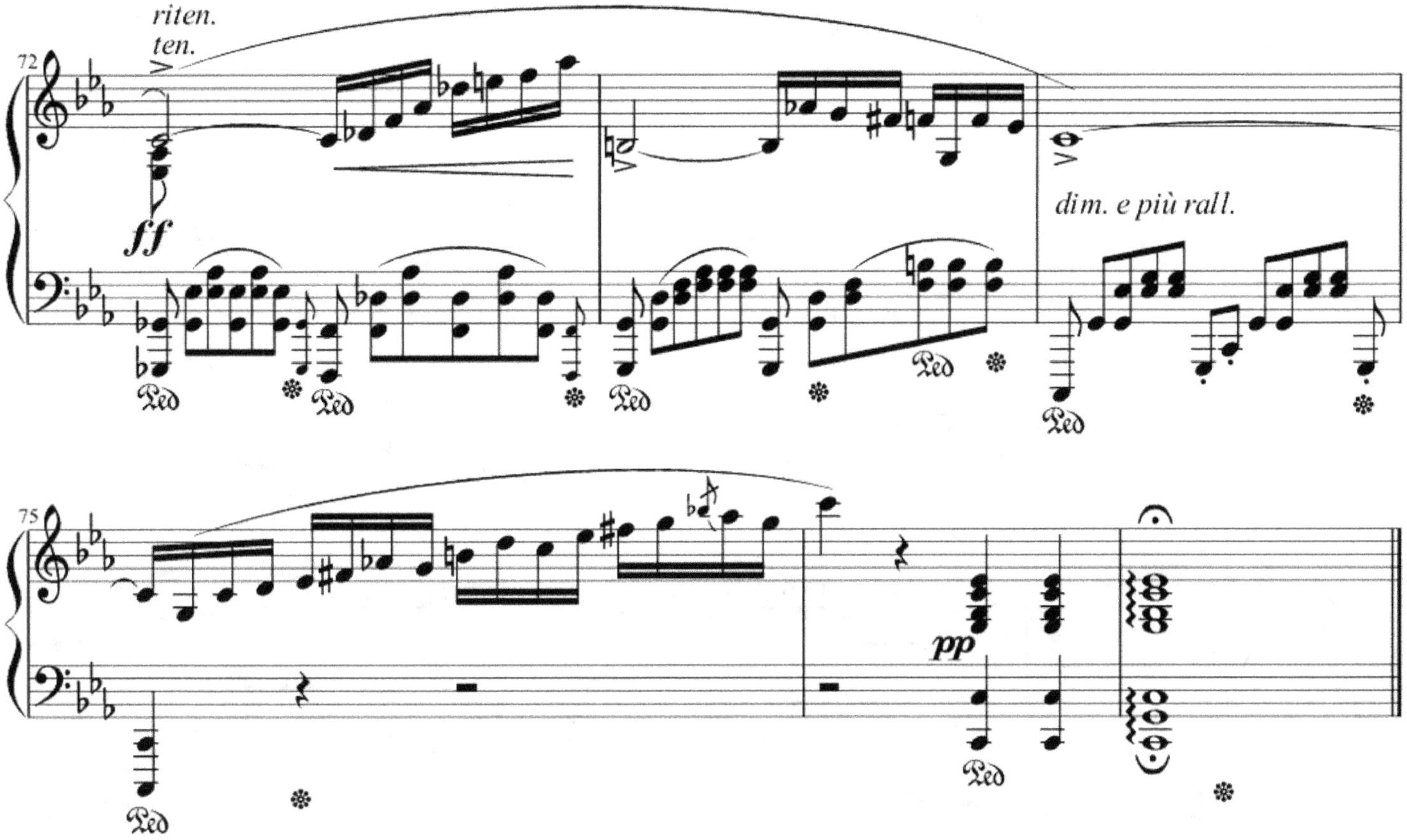
72
riten.
ten.
ff
dim. e più rall.
75
pp

Nocturne in F# Major

Opus 15, No 2

Frédéric François Chopin

pp e poco ritenuto
con fuoco
stringendo
ritenuto
m.g.
Doppio movimento
cresc.
f

37
cresc.
41
dim.
dim.
f
45
Tempo I
pp
dim.
molto rallentando
smorz.
dolce
49
7
52
con forza
sf
tr

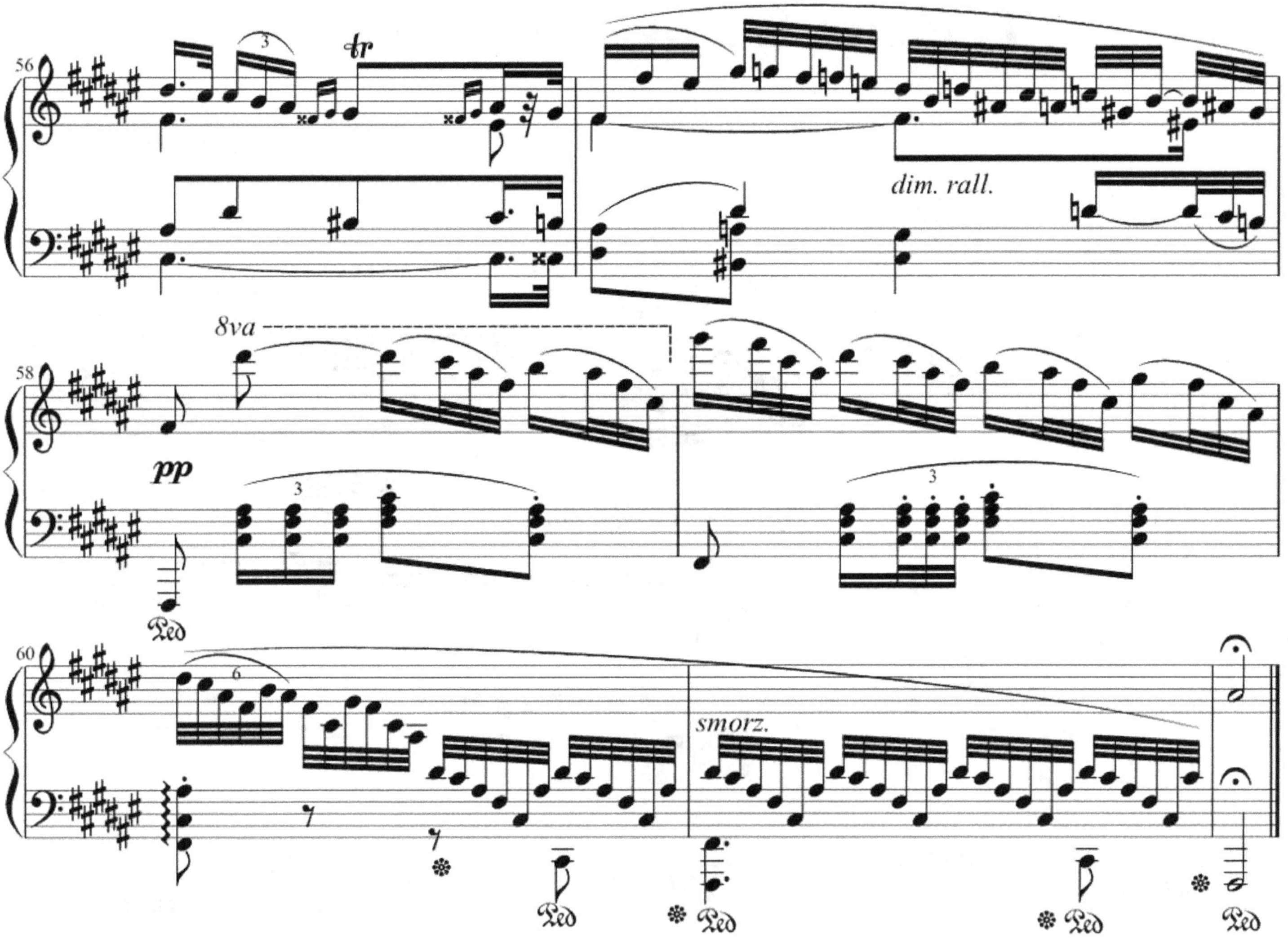
56
tr
3
dim. rall.
58
8va
pp
Ped
60
6
smorz.

Toccata & Fugue in D minor

Johann Sebastian Bach

rall.
Allegro
pp légèrement
cresc.
ff
m.g.
Large
poco rit.
à l'aise
allargando

Prestissimo
p
rall.
Maestoso
allargando
ff
rit.
FUGA
♩ = 84
calme et simple
p

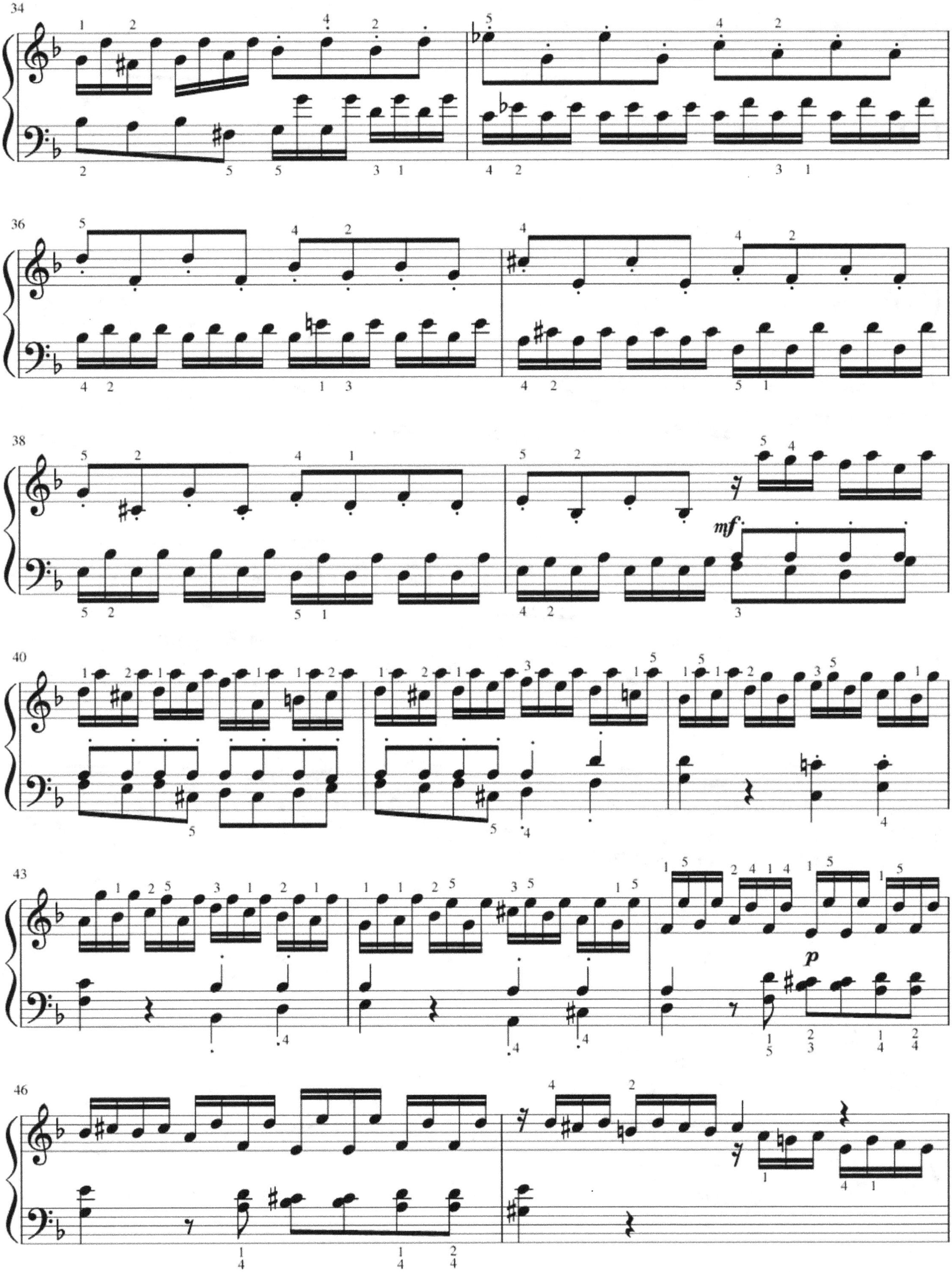
mf
p

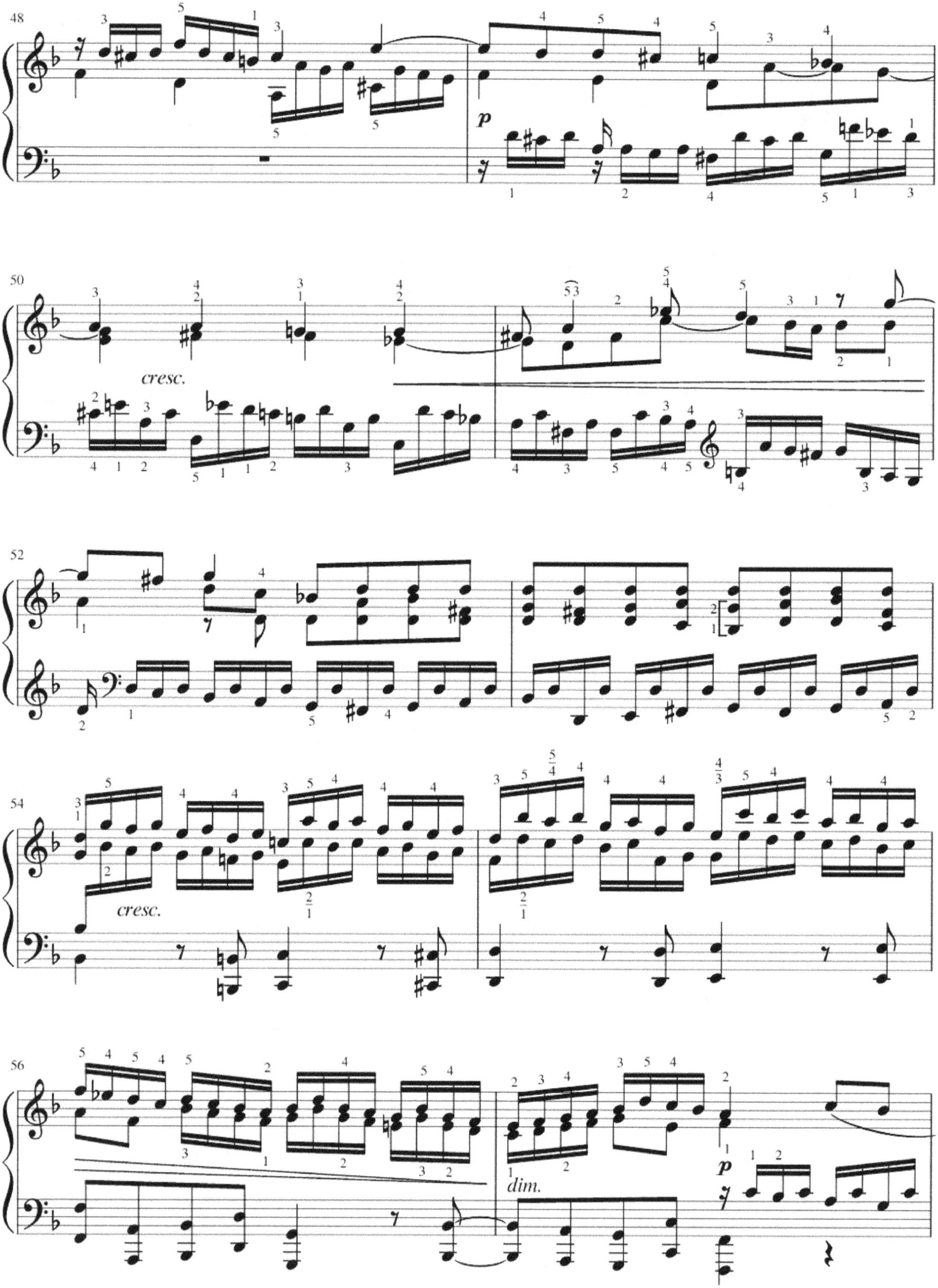
48
p
50
cresc.
52
54
cresc.
56
dim.
p

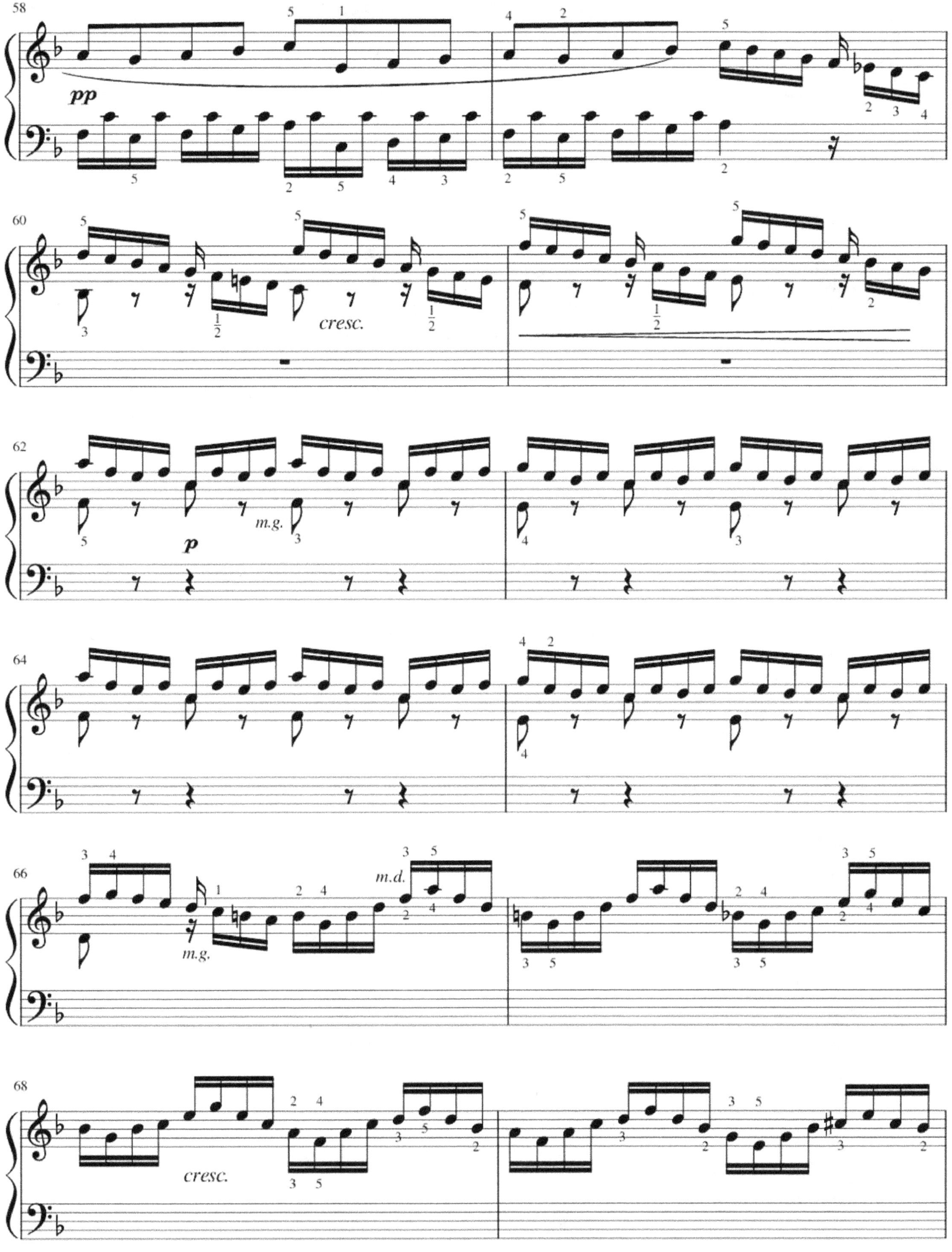
58
pp
60
cresc.
62
p
m.g.
64
66
m.g.
m.d.
68
cresc.

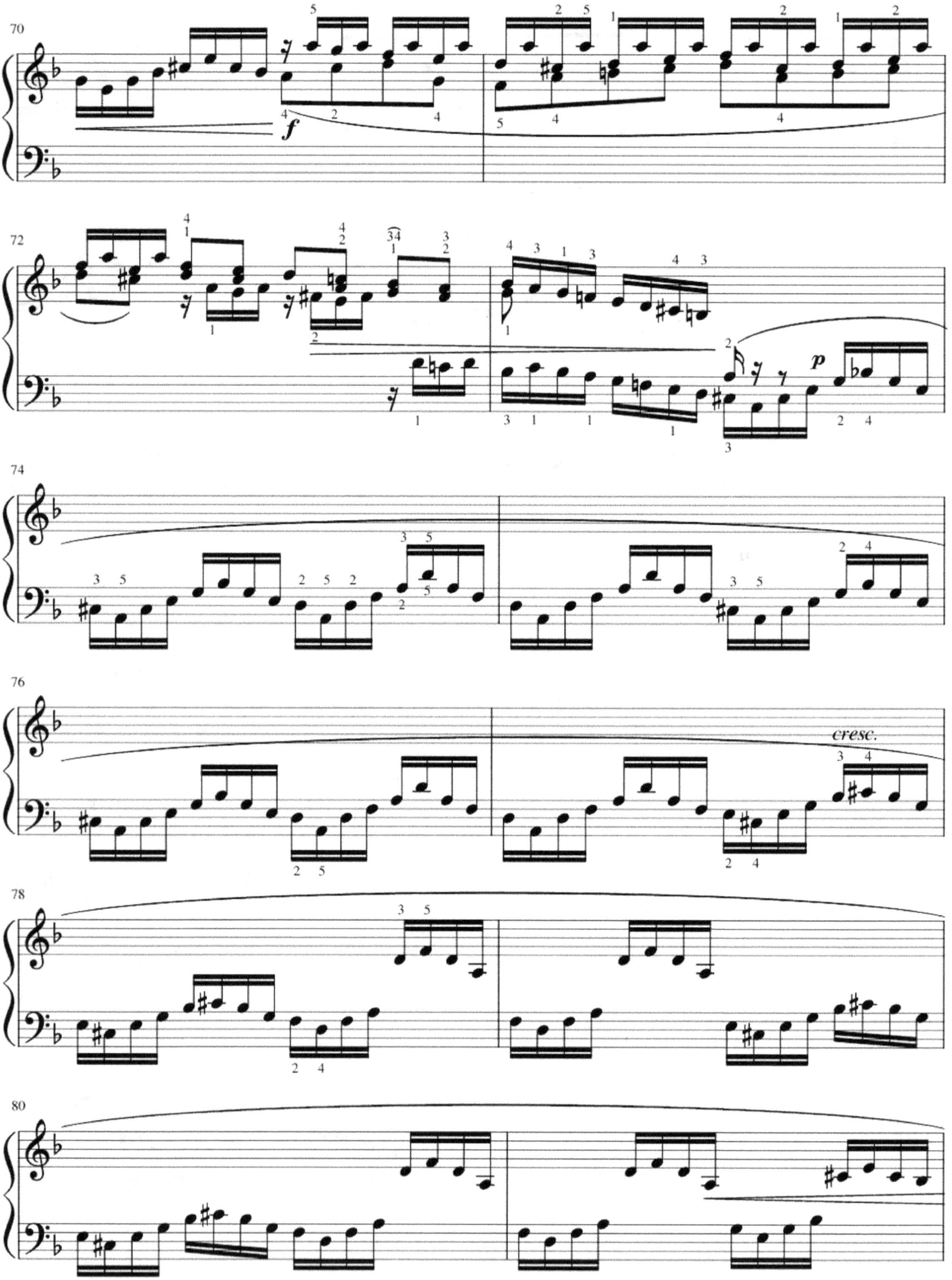
cresc.

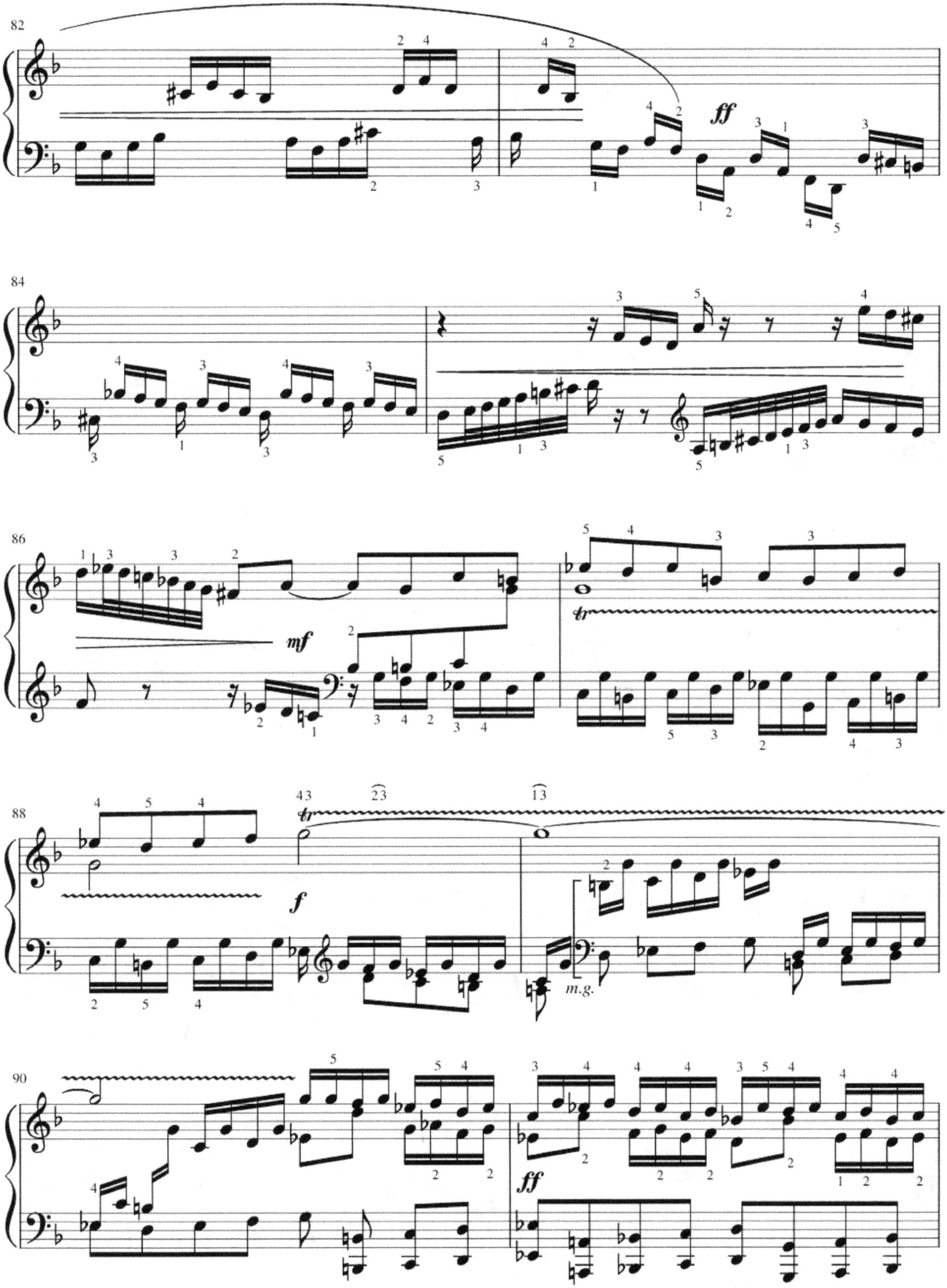
82
ff
84
86
mf
88
f
m.g.
90
ff

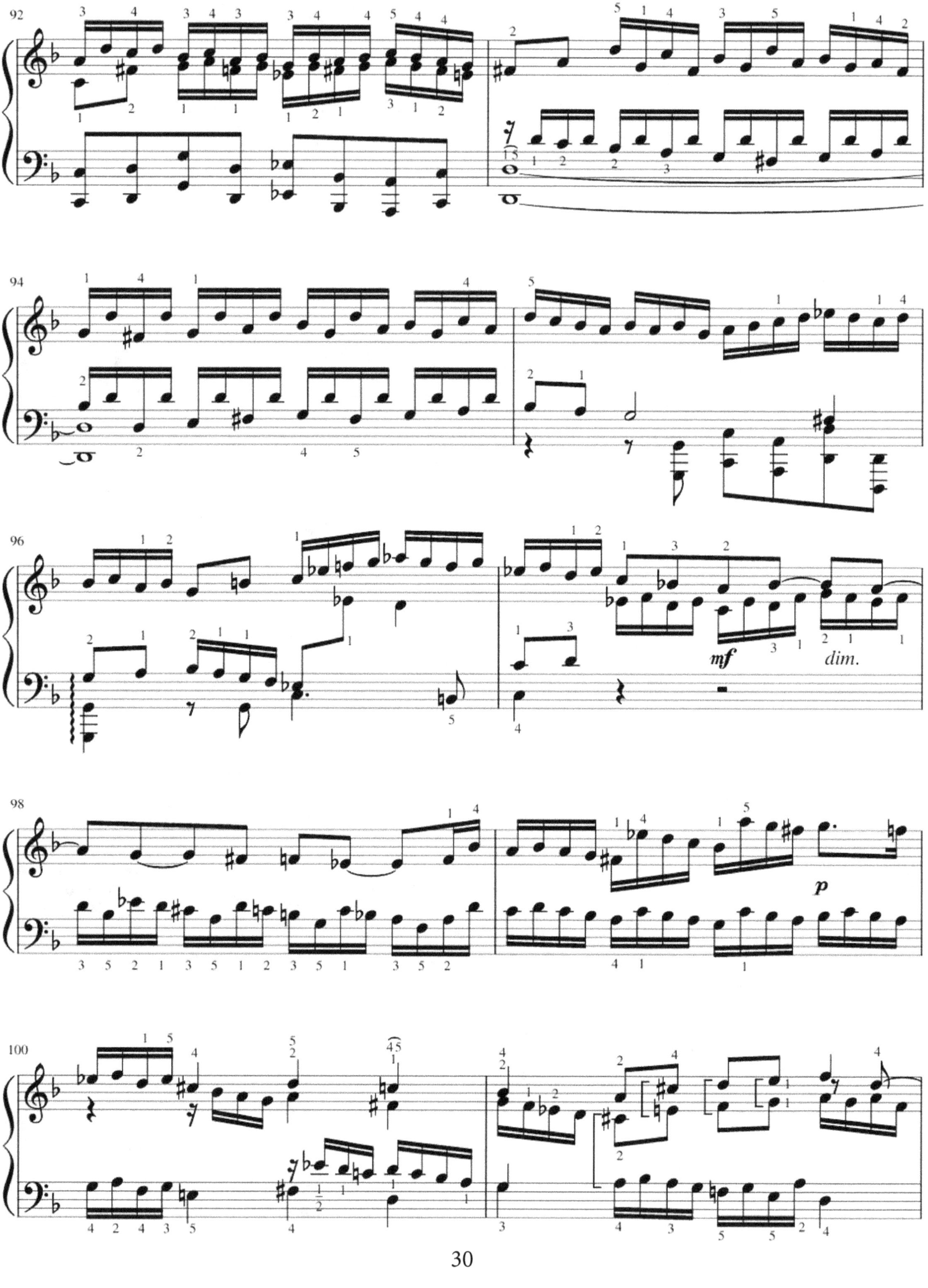
92
94
96
98
100
mf
dim.
p

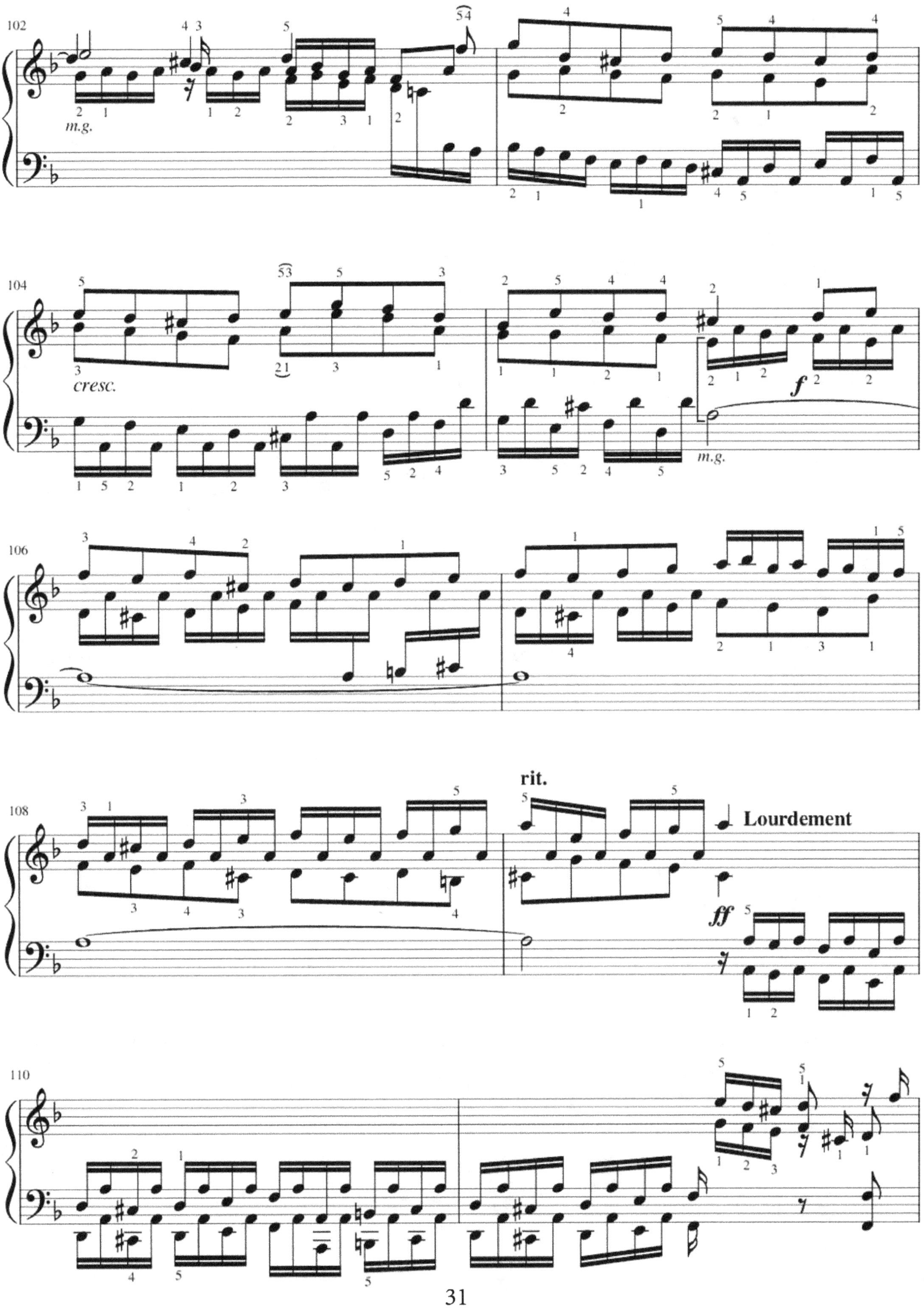
102
m.g.
104
cresc.
m.g.
106
108
rit.
Lourdement
110

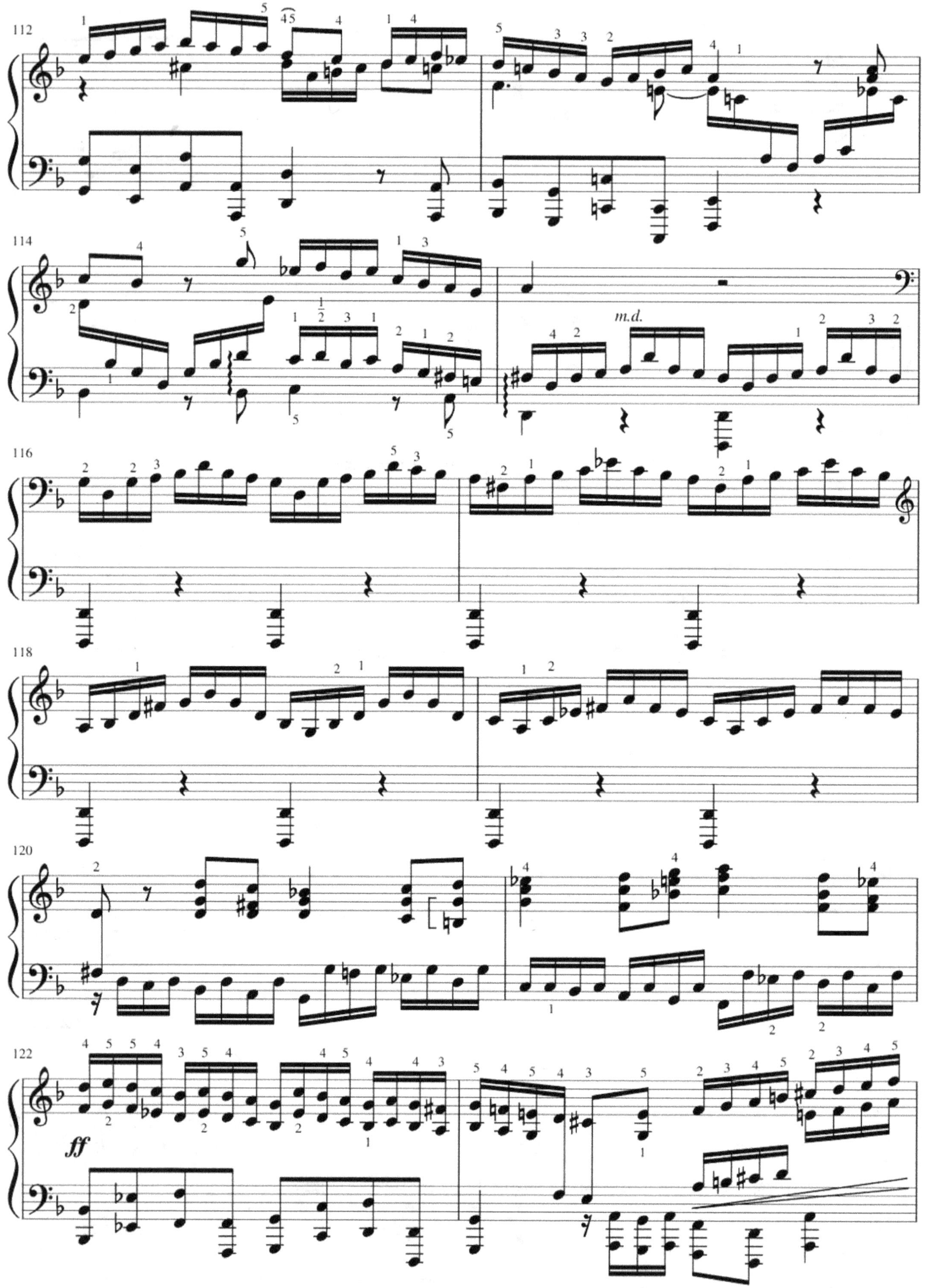
112
114
m.d.
116
118
120
122
ff

124
ff
m.g.
126
allargando
recitativo
8
128
129
fff
m.d.
131
Très largement
Presto
f
m.g.

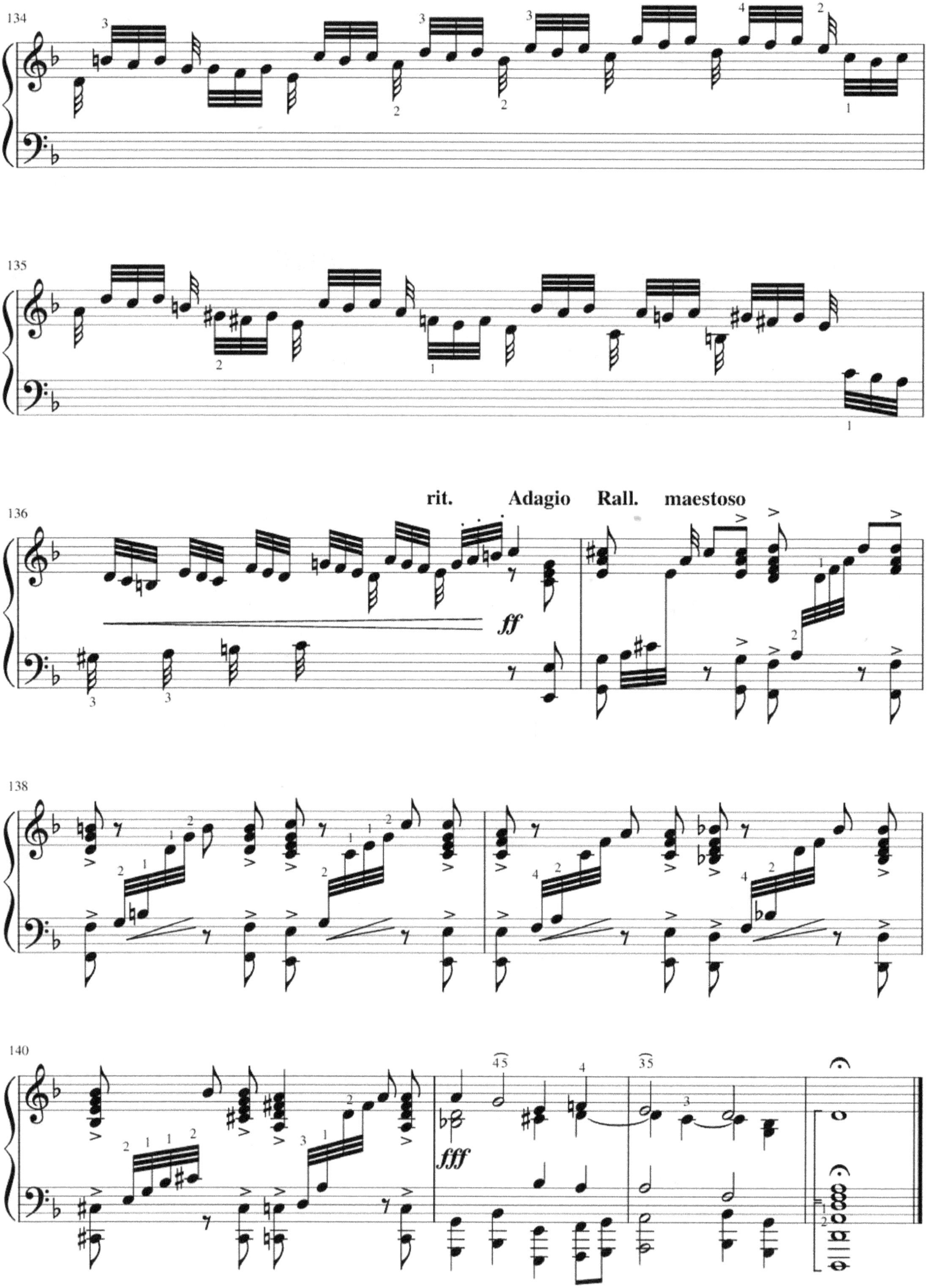
134
135
rit.
Adagio
Rall.
maestoso
136
ff
138
140
fff

The Lark

Mikhail Ivanovich Glinka

35

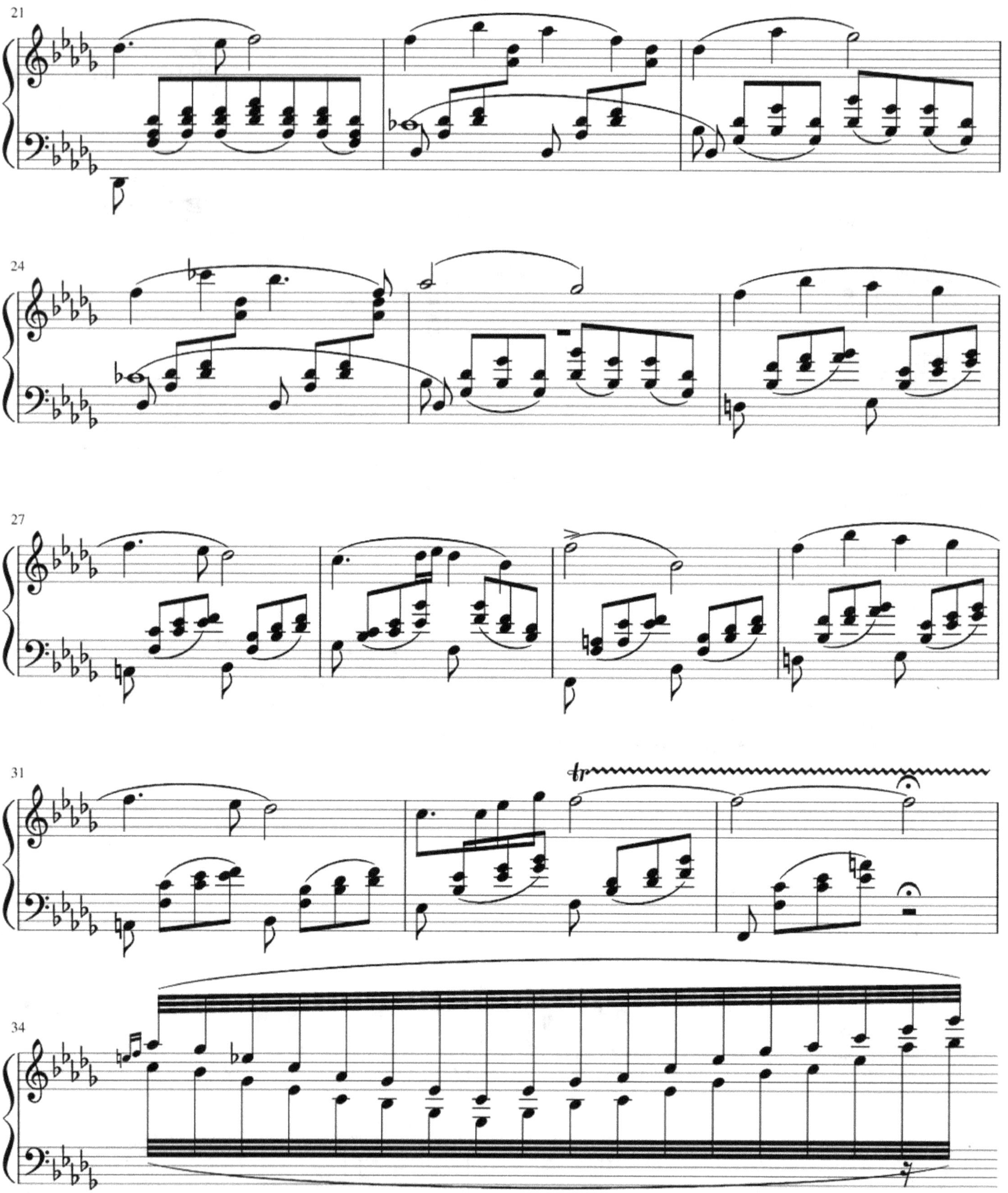
21
24
27
31
tr
34

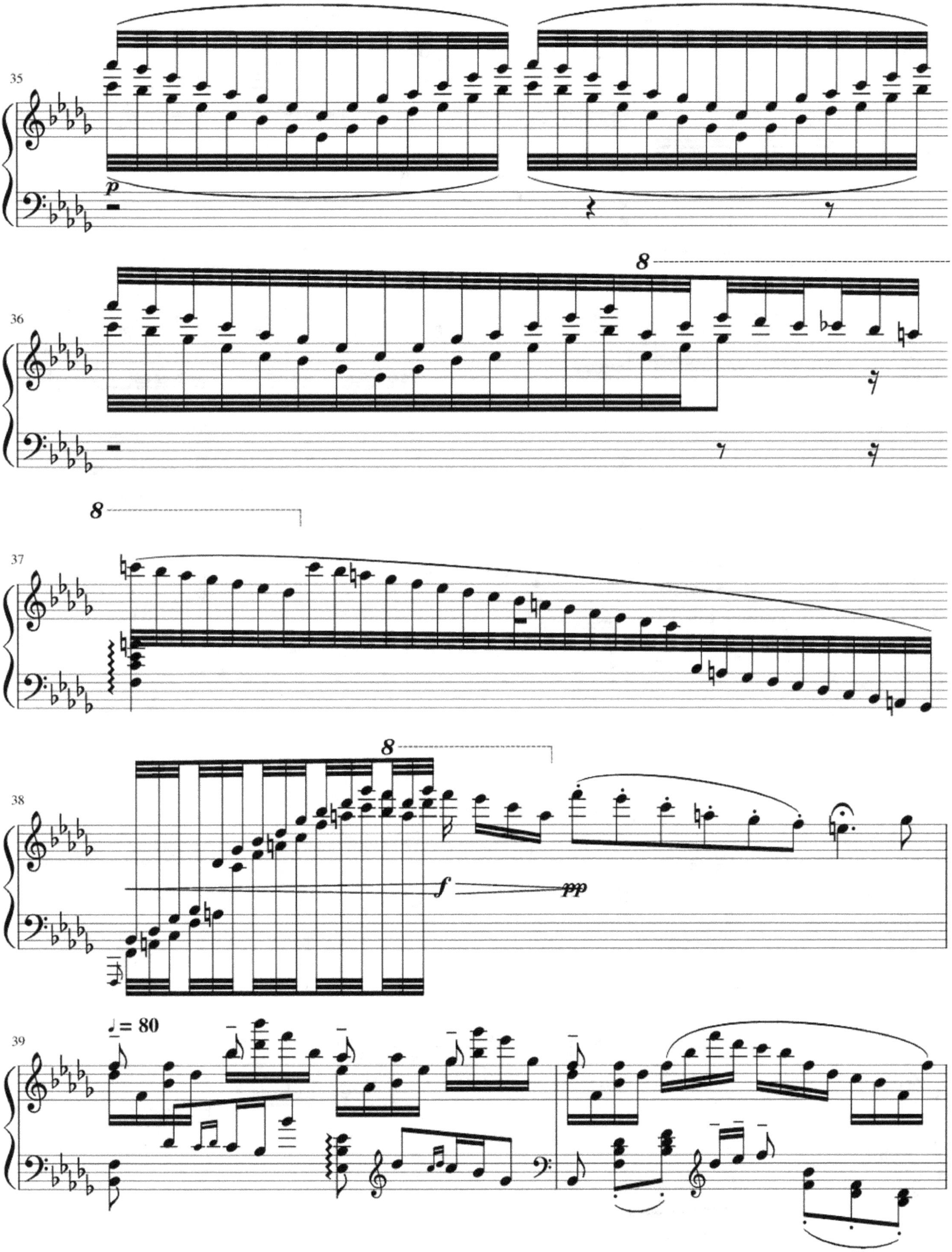
35
p
36
8
37
8
38
8
f
pp
39
♩ = 80

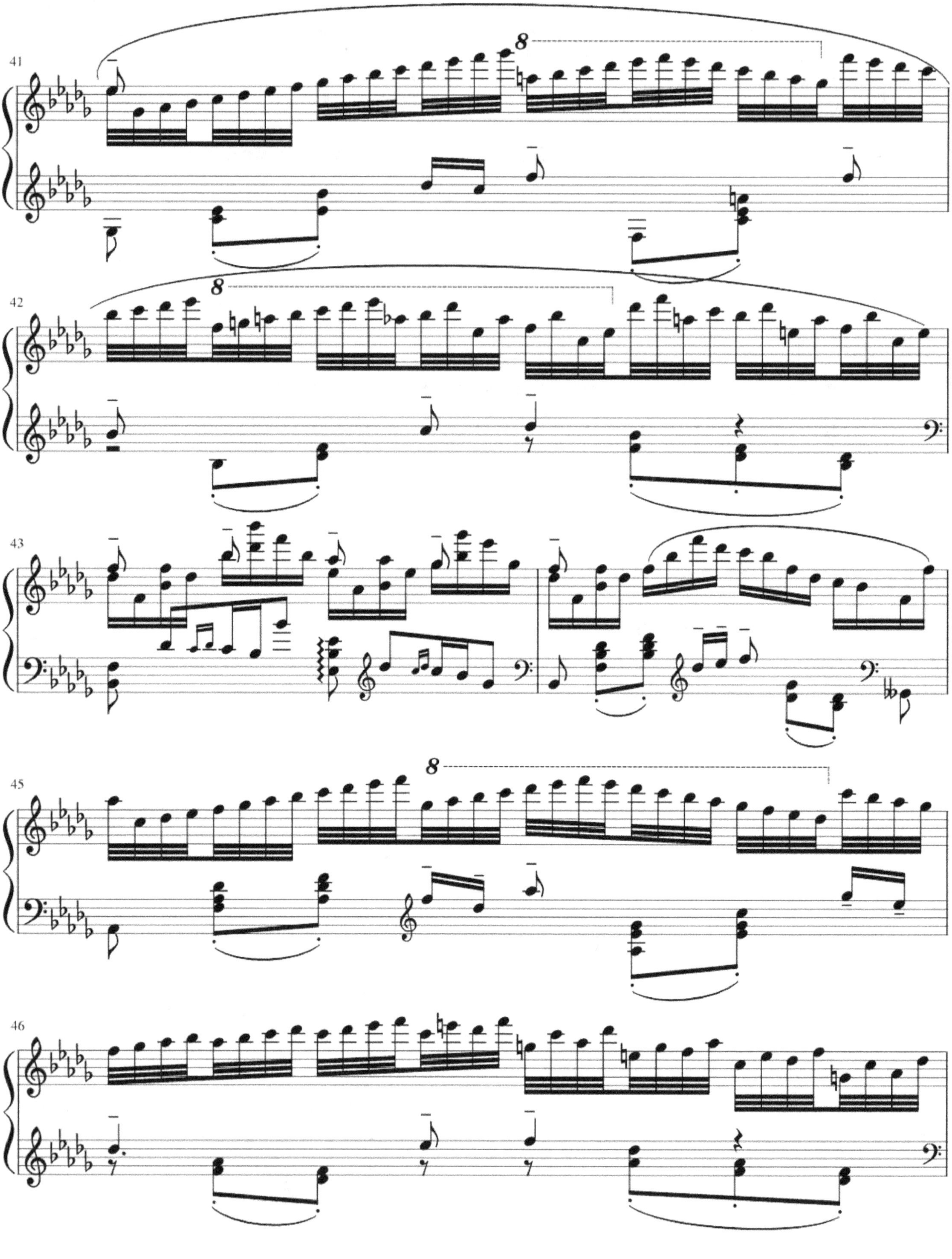
41
8
42
8
43
45
8
46

GRADE 8

Waltz in B Minor
Opus 69, No 2

Frédéric François Chopin

44

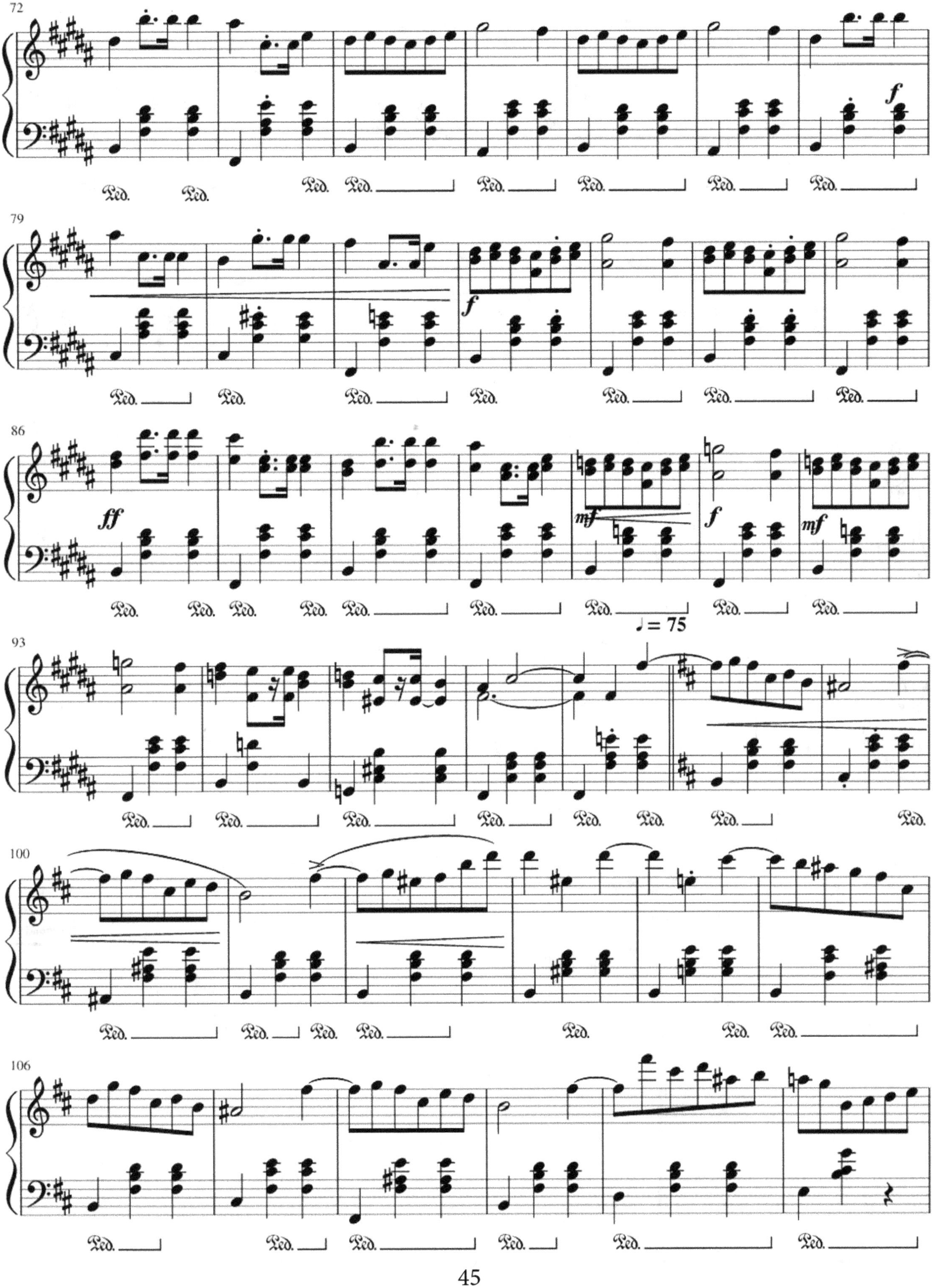
72
79
86
93
100
106
♩ = 75
f
ff
mf
Ped.

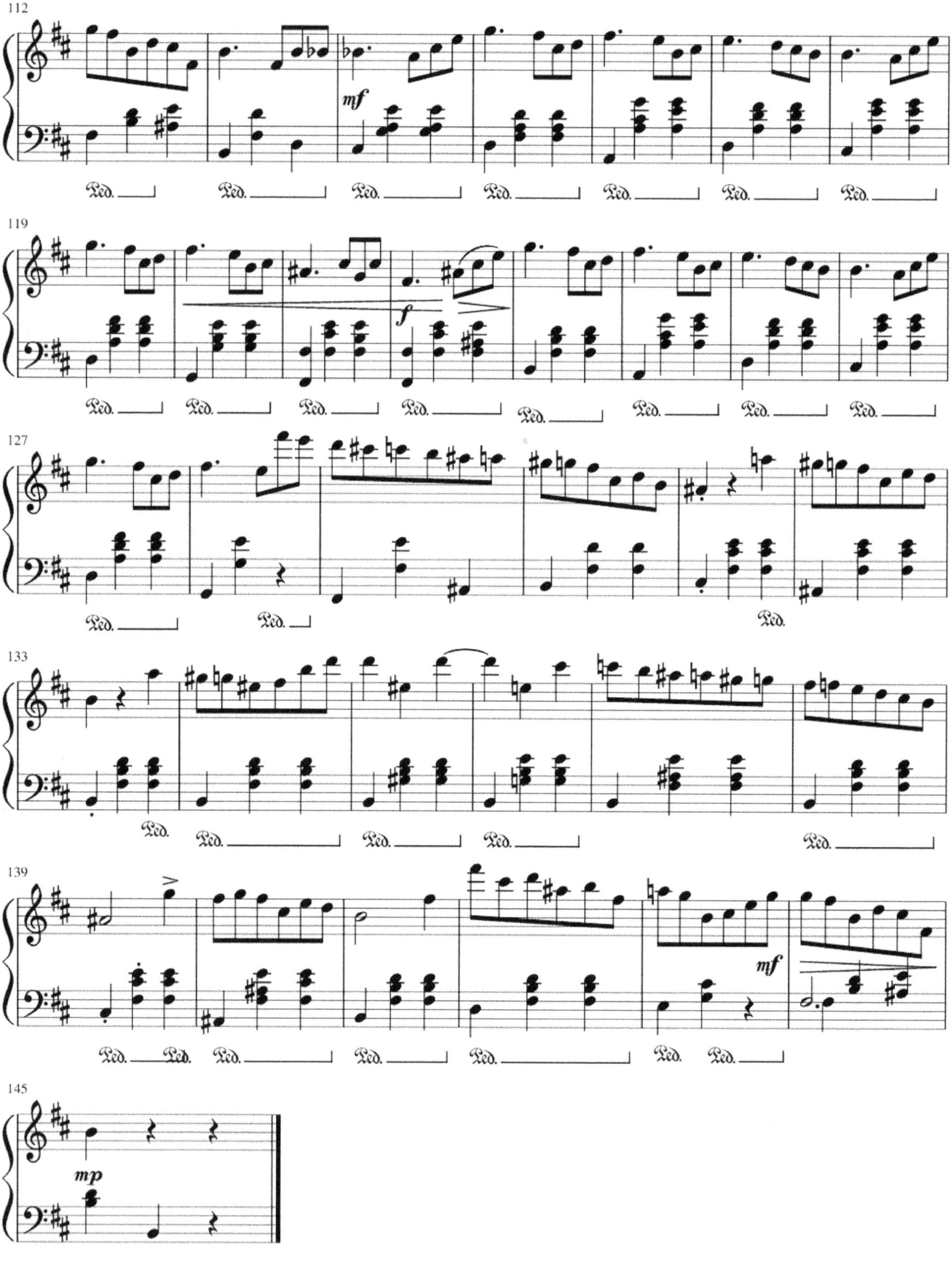
112
mf
Ped.
119
f
127
133
139
mf
145
mp

Fugue in B♭ Minor
HWV 607

George Frideric Handel

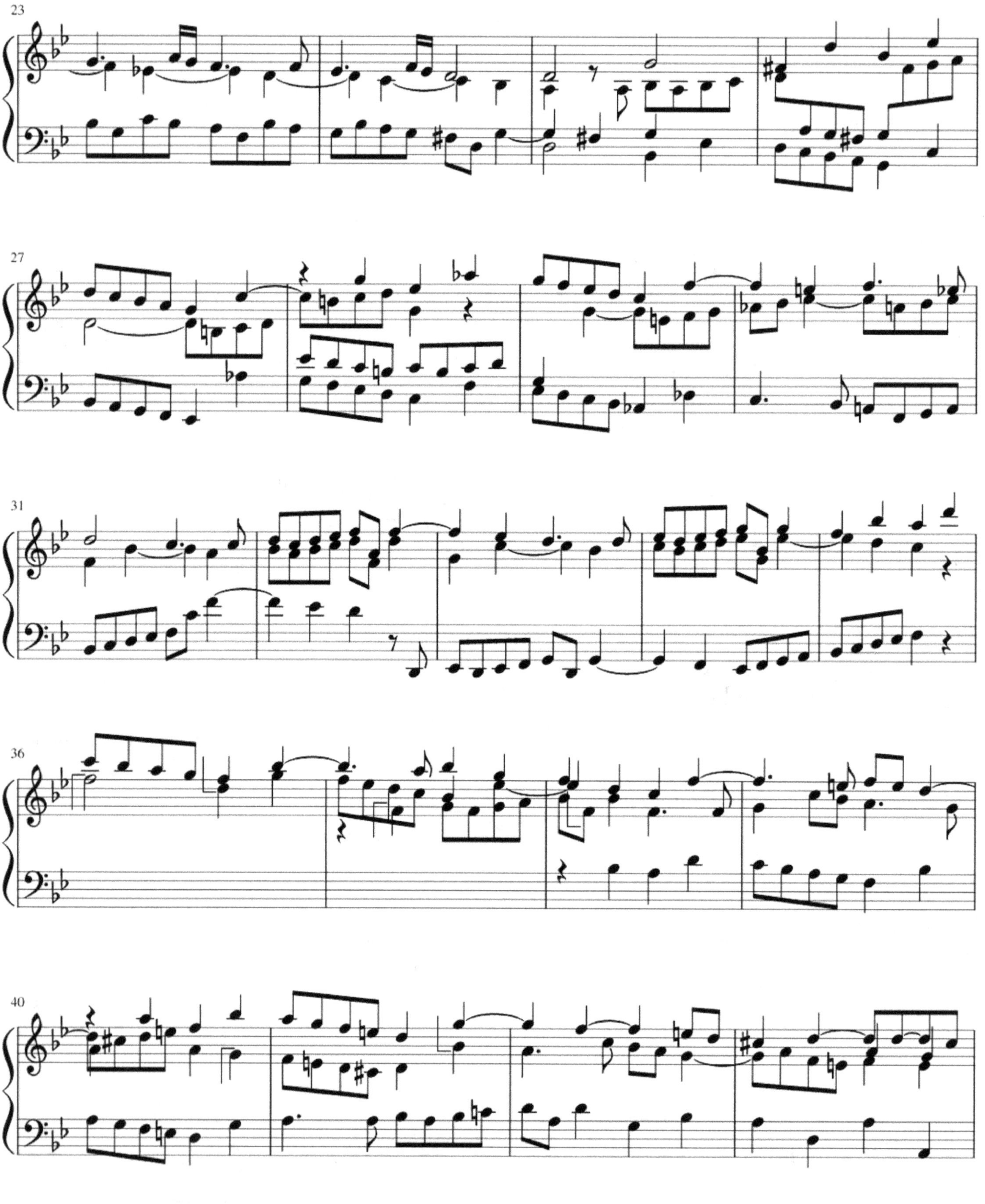
23
27
31
36
40

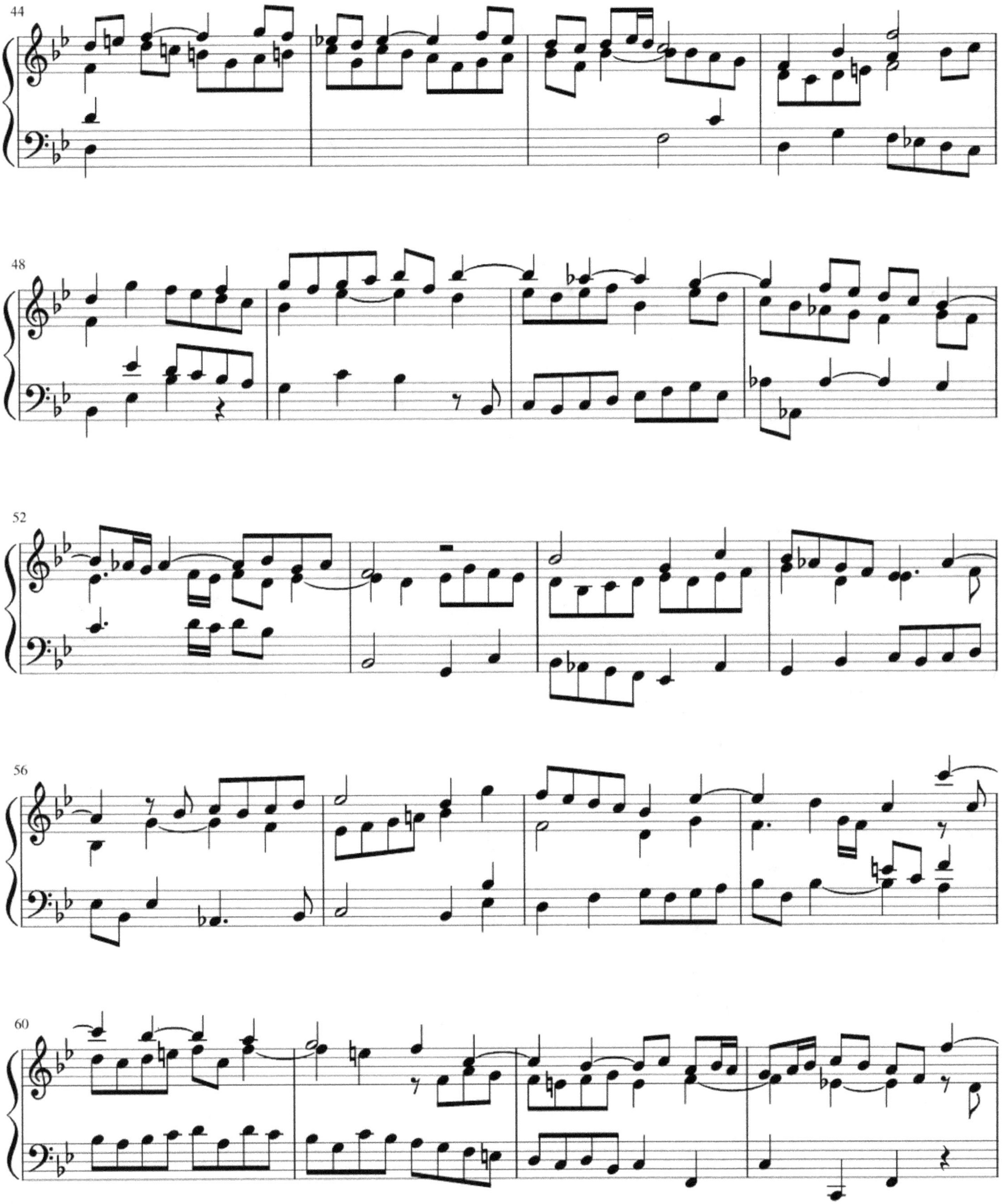
44
48
52
56
60

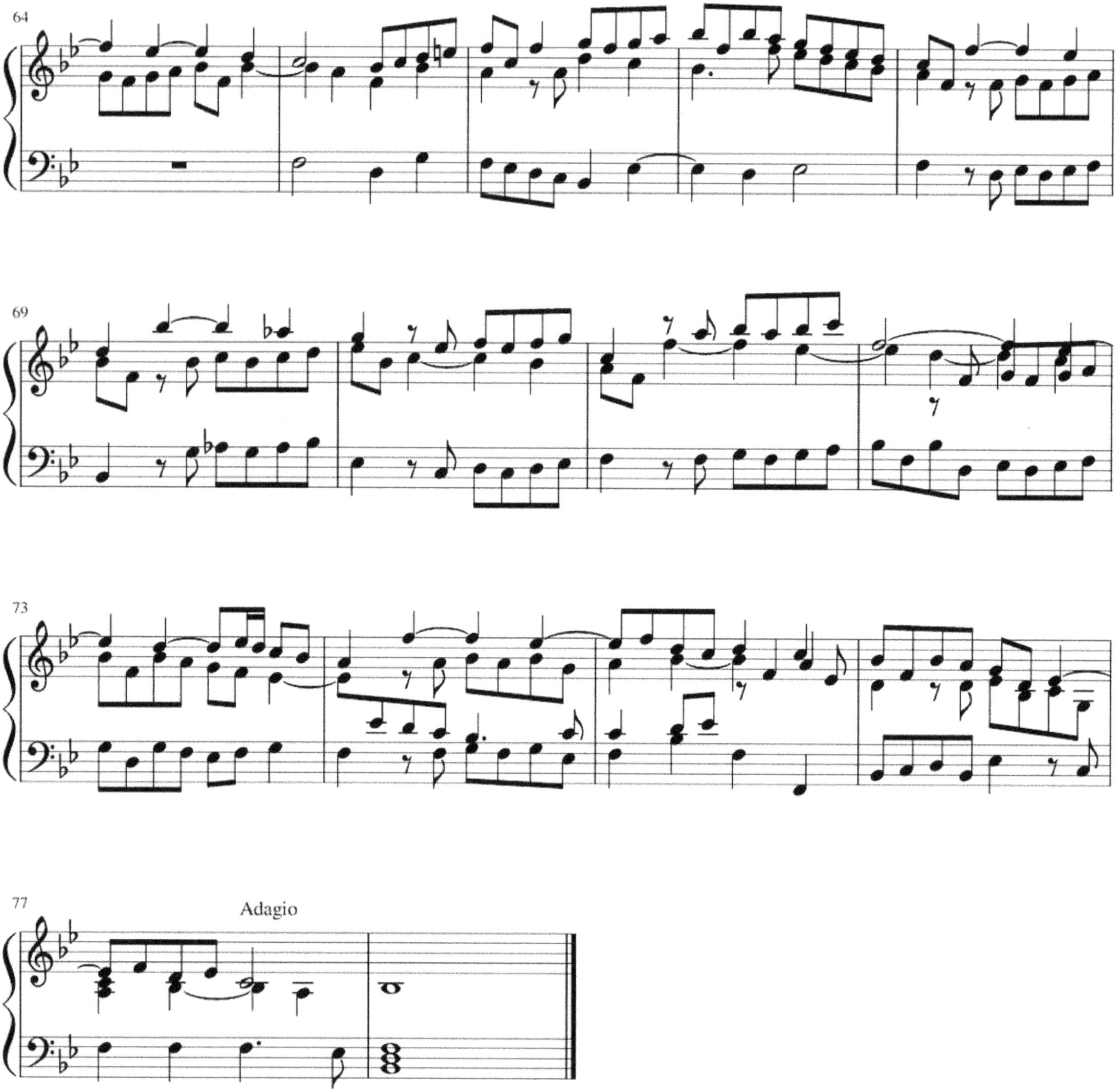
64
69
73
77
Adagio

Sonata in E Major

Kp.162, L.21

Giuseppe Domenico Scarlatti

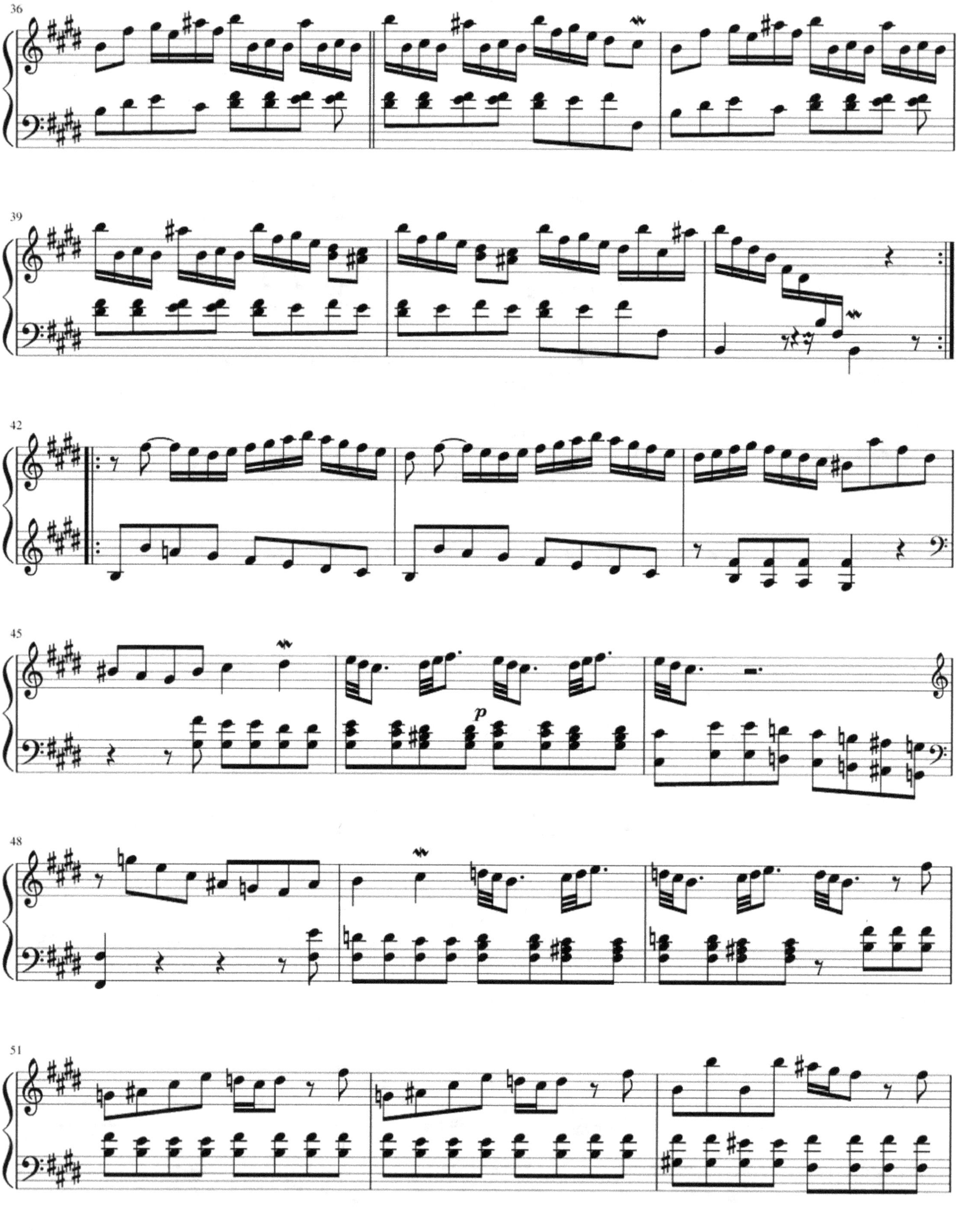
36
39
42
45
p
48
51

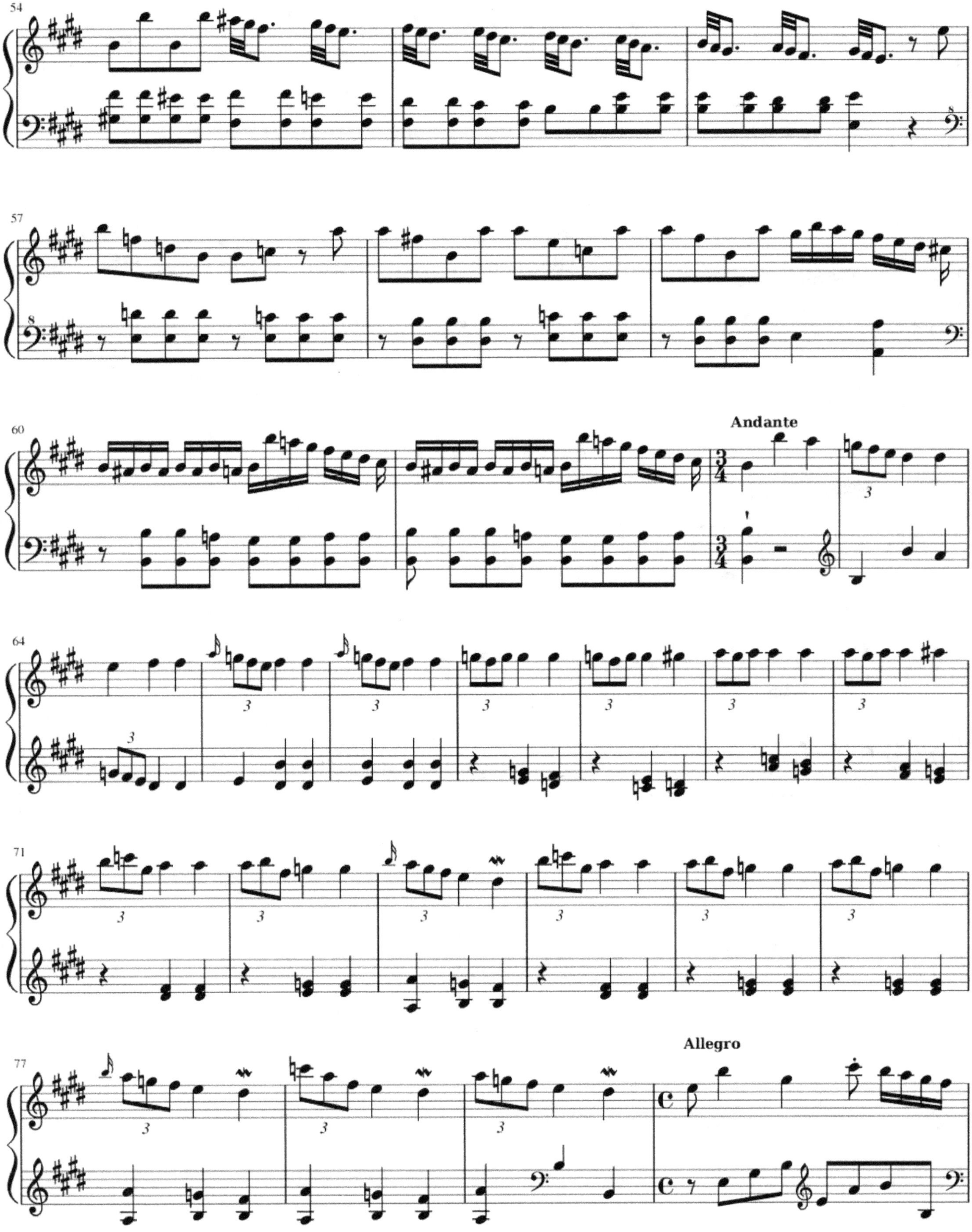
Andante
Allegro

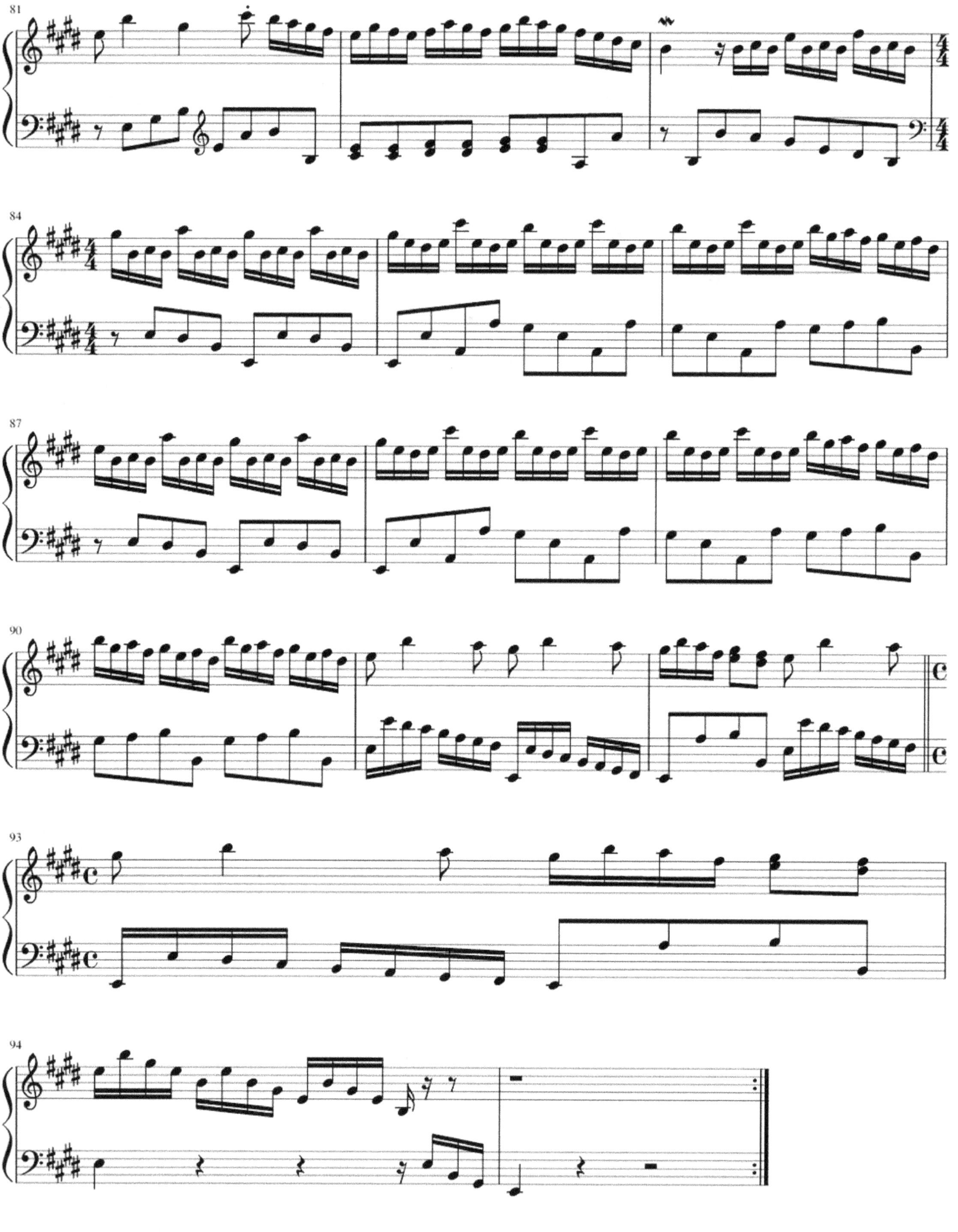
81
84
87
90
93
94

French Suite No 5

Gigue

Johann Sebastian Bach

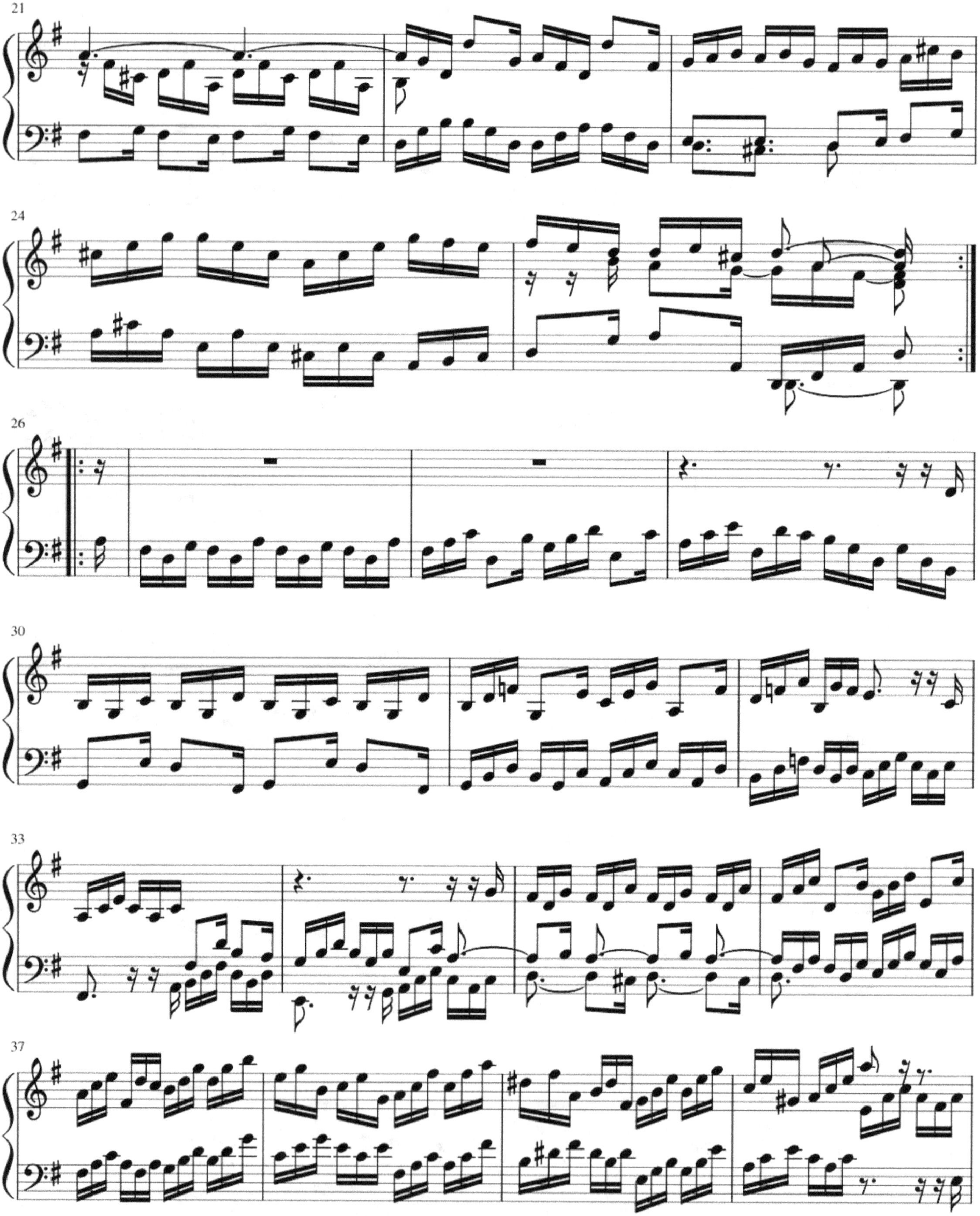
21
24
26
30
33
37

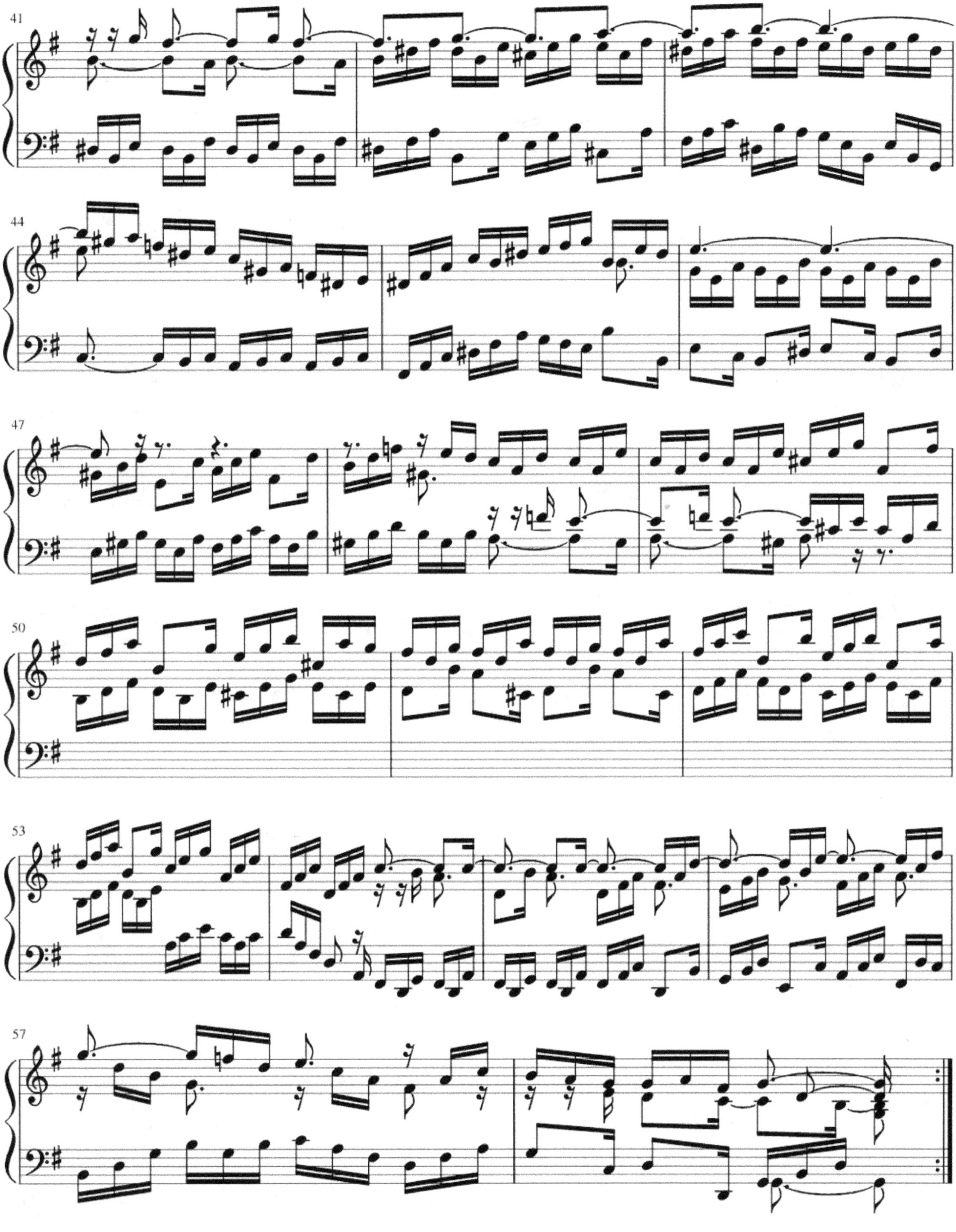
41
44
47
50
53
57

Prelude and Fugue in D Minor
BWV 875

Johann Sebastian Bach

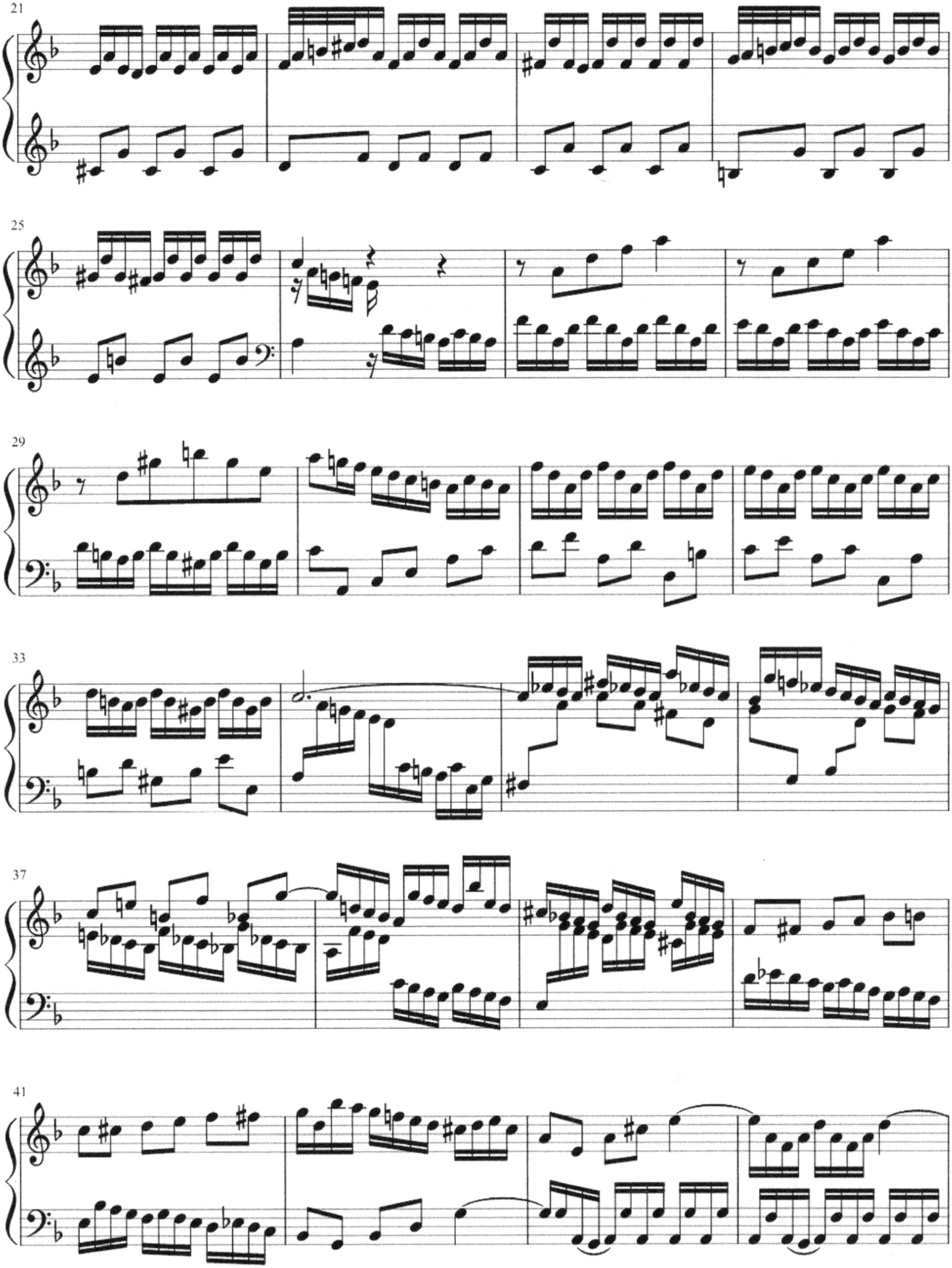
21
25
29
33
37
41

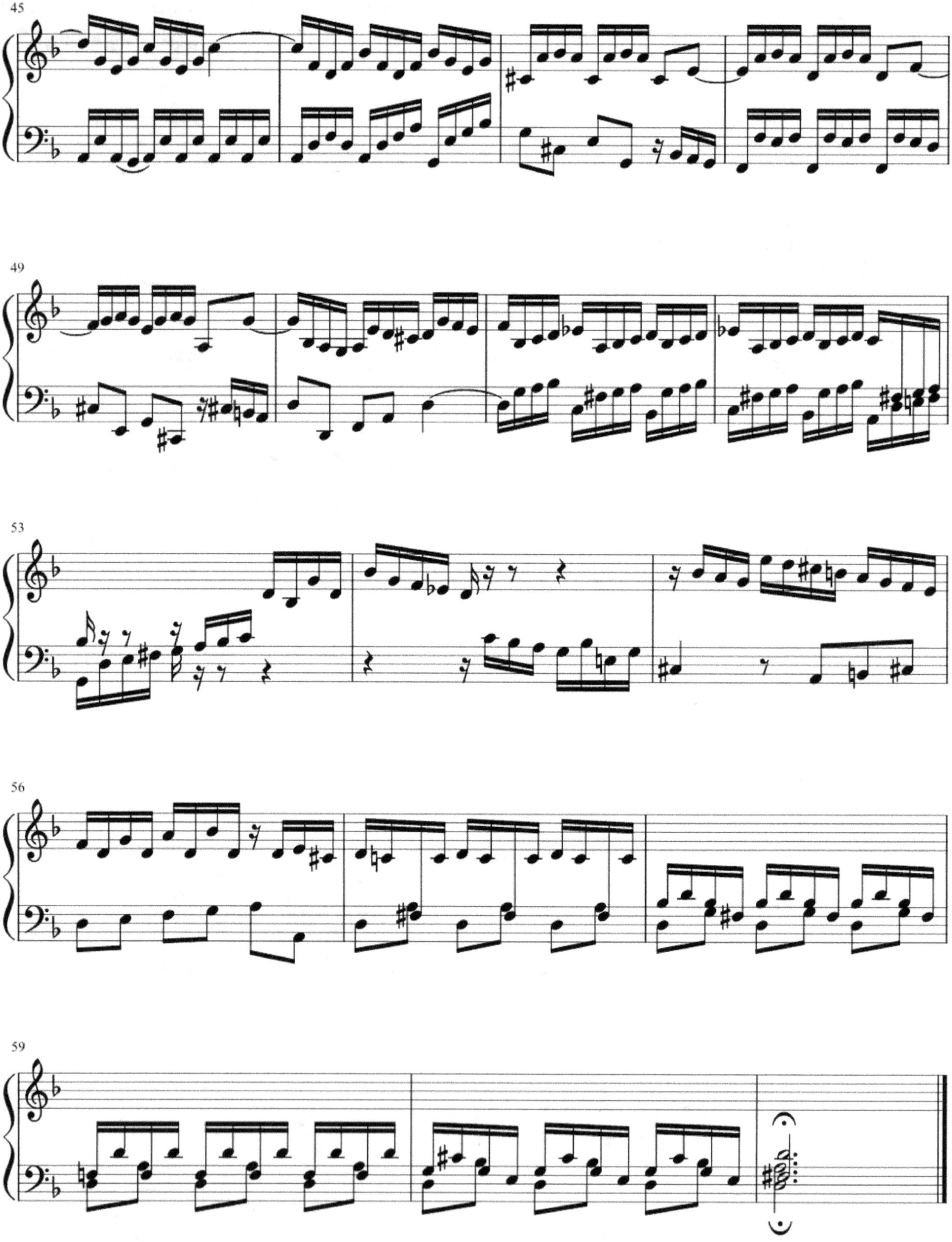
45
49
53
56
59

Sonata in F Minor
Opus 2, No 1

Ludwig Van Beethoven

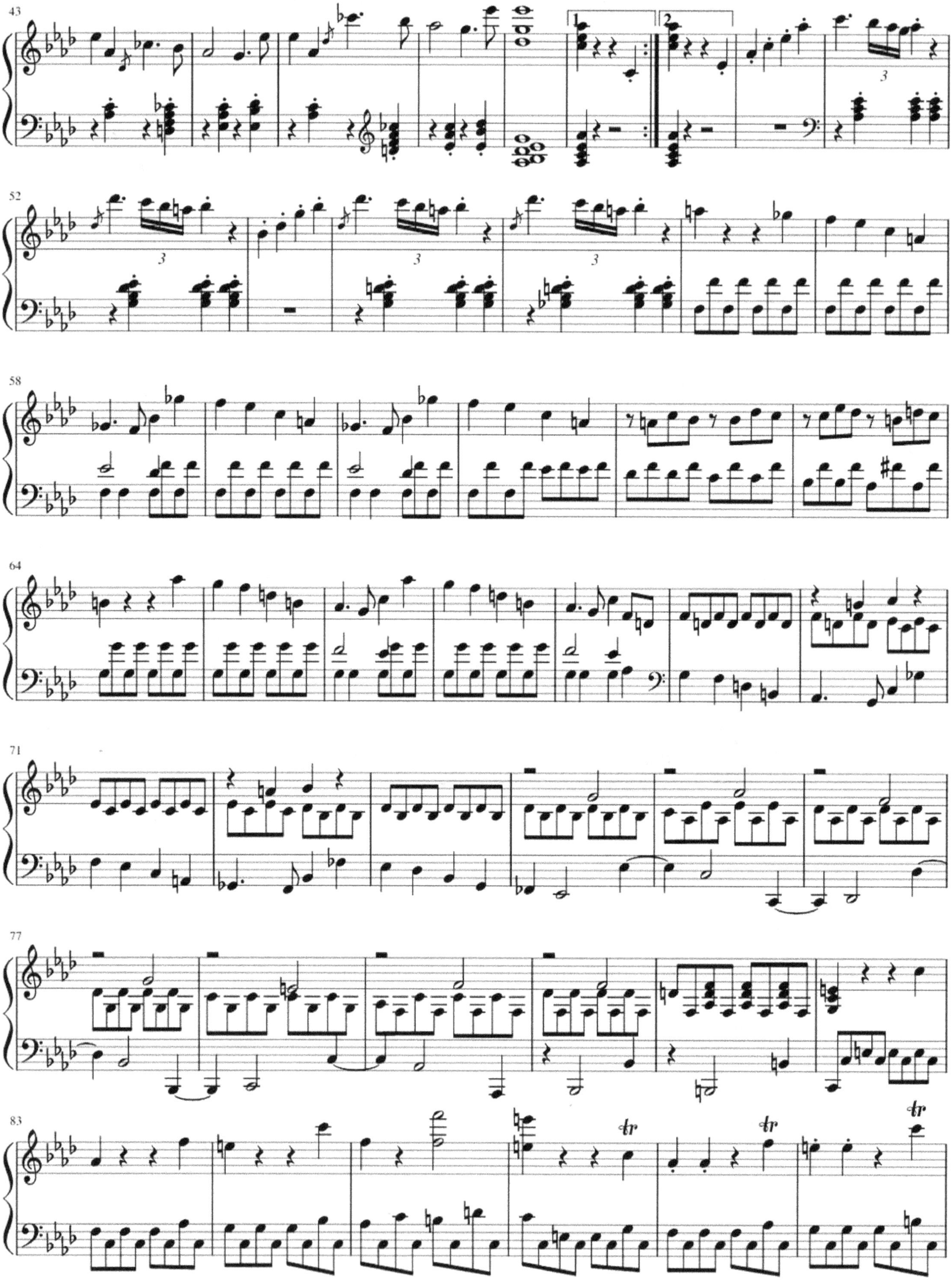
43
1
2
3
52
3
3
3
58
64
71
77
83
tr
tr
tr

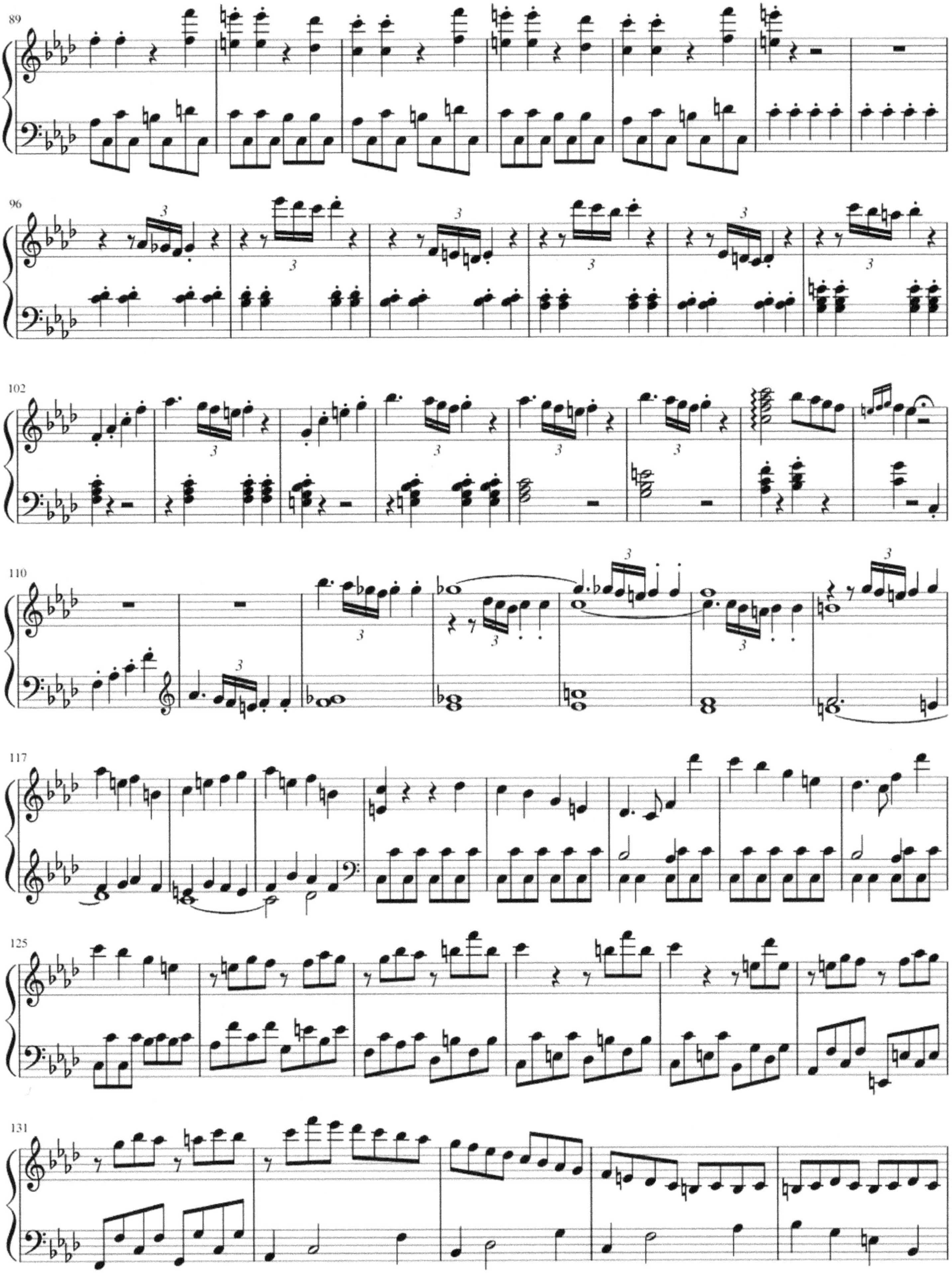
89
96
102
110
117
125
131

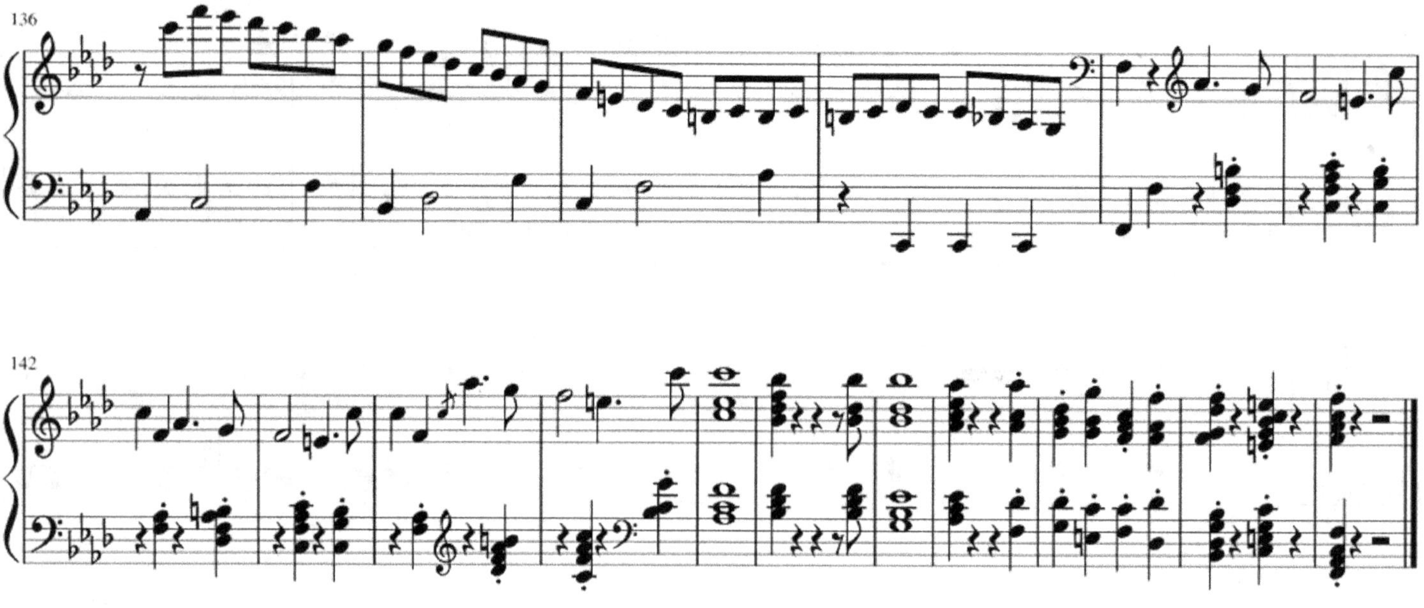
136
142

Sonata in C
K.279, 1st Movement, Allegro

Wolfgang Amadeus Mozart

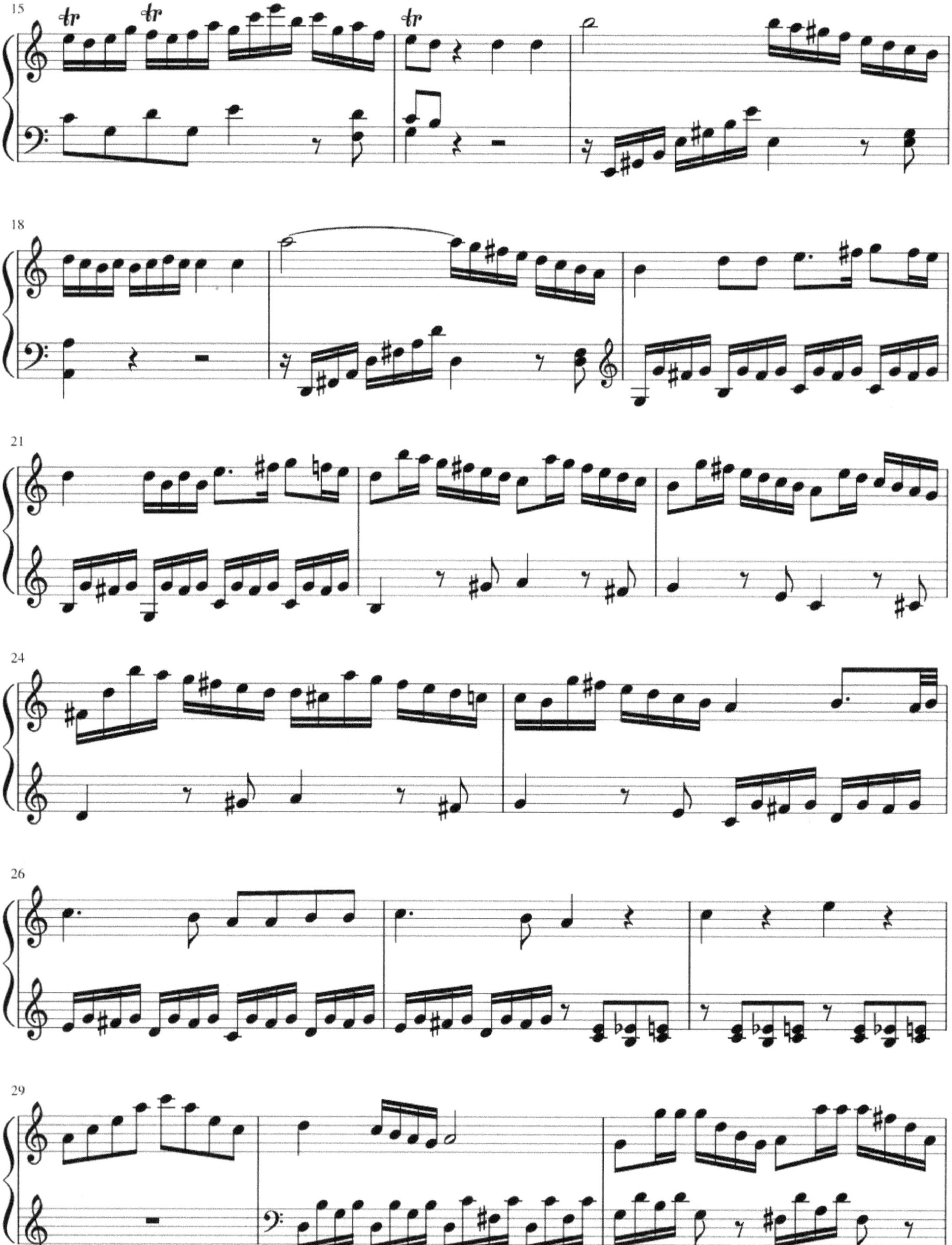
15
tr
tr
tr
18
21
24
26
29

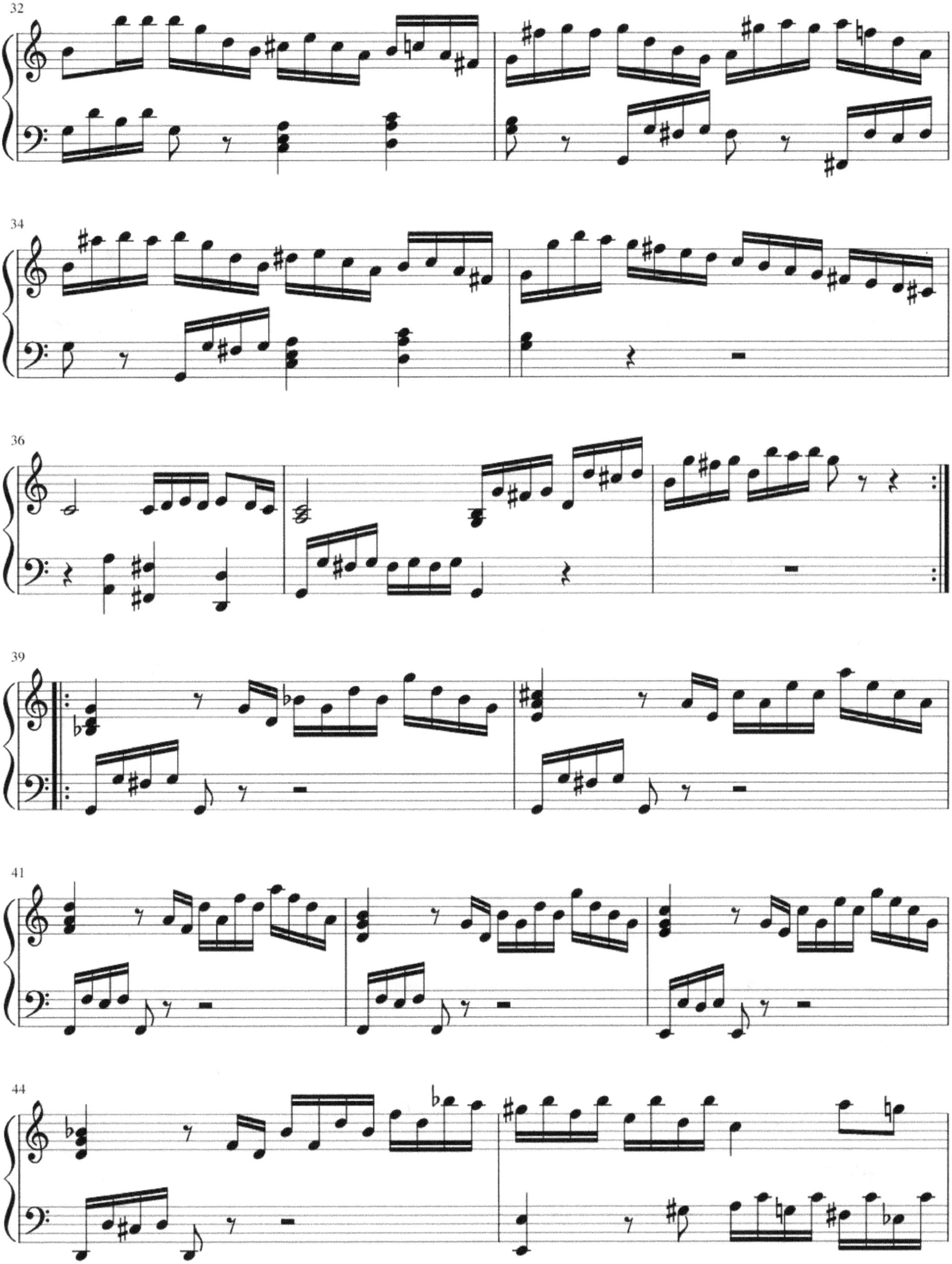
32
34
36
39
41
44

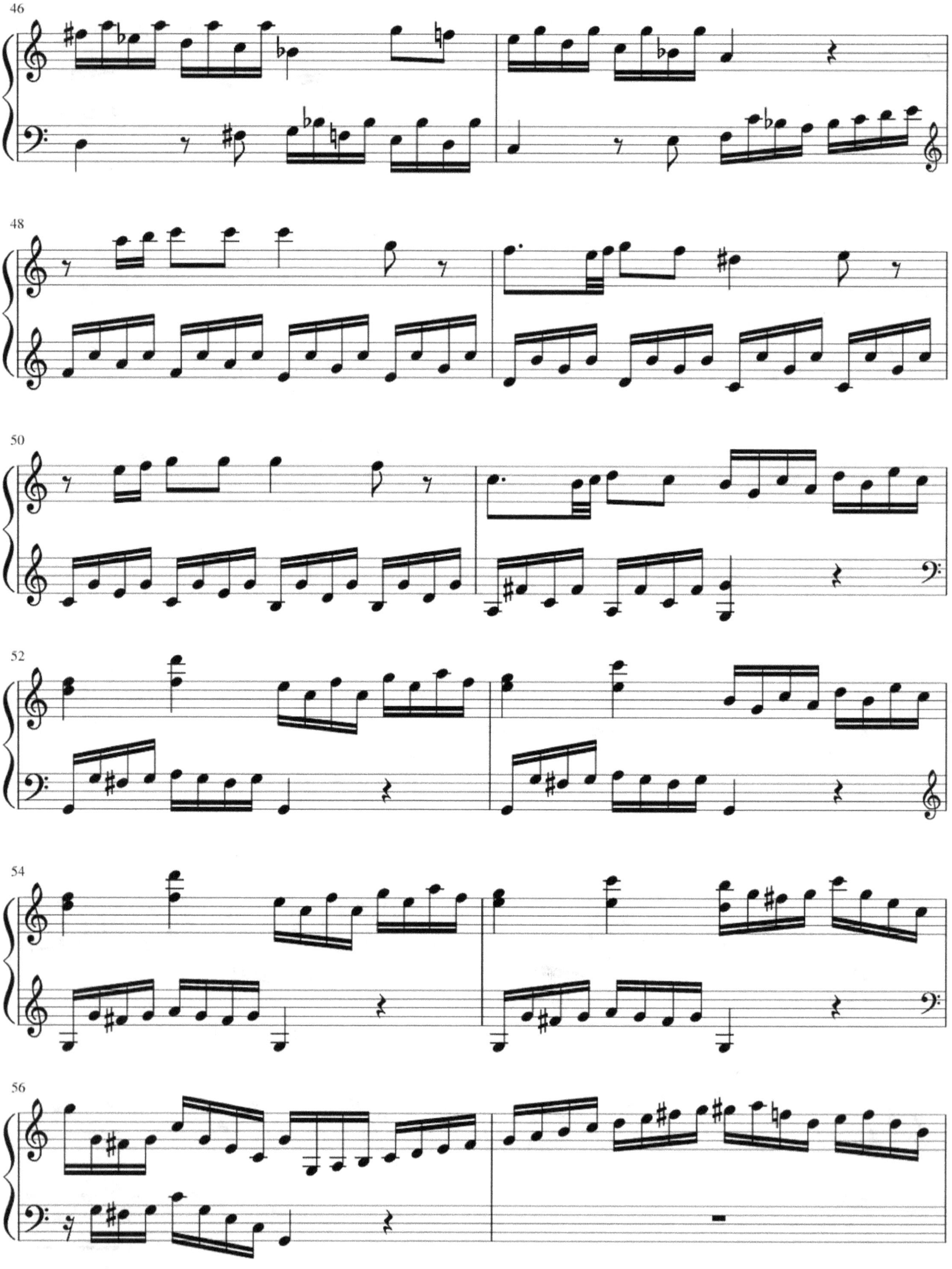
46
48
50
52
54
56

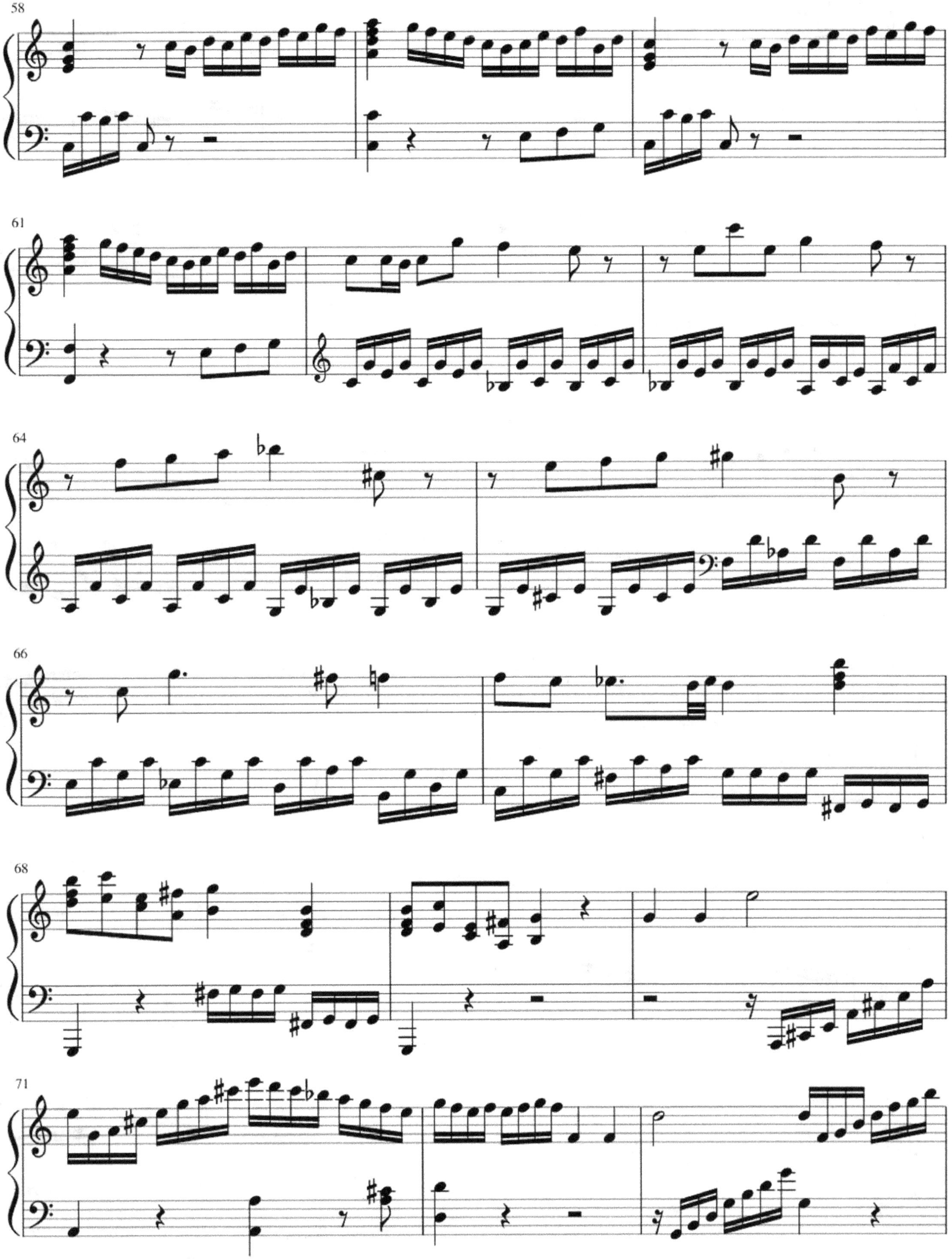
58
61
64
66
68
71

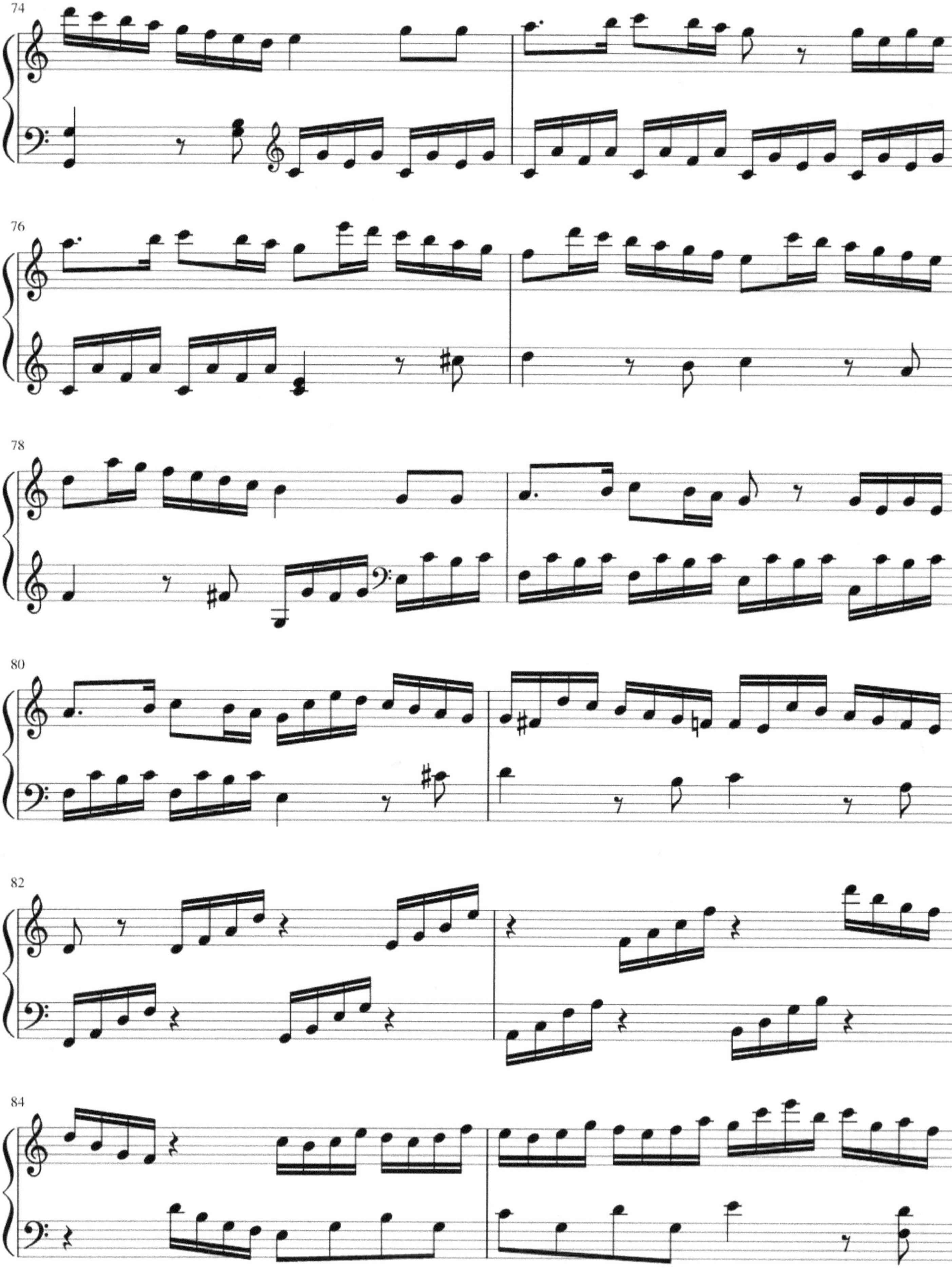
74
76
78
80
82
84

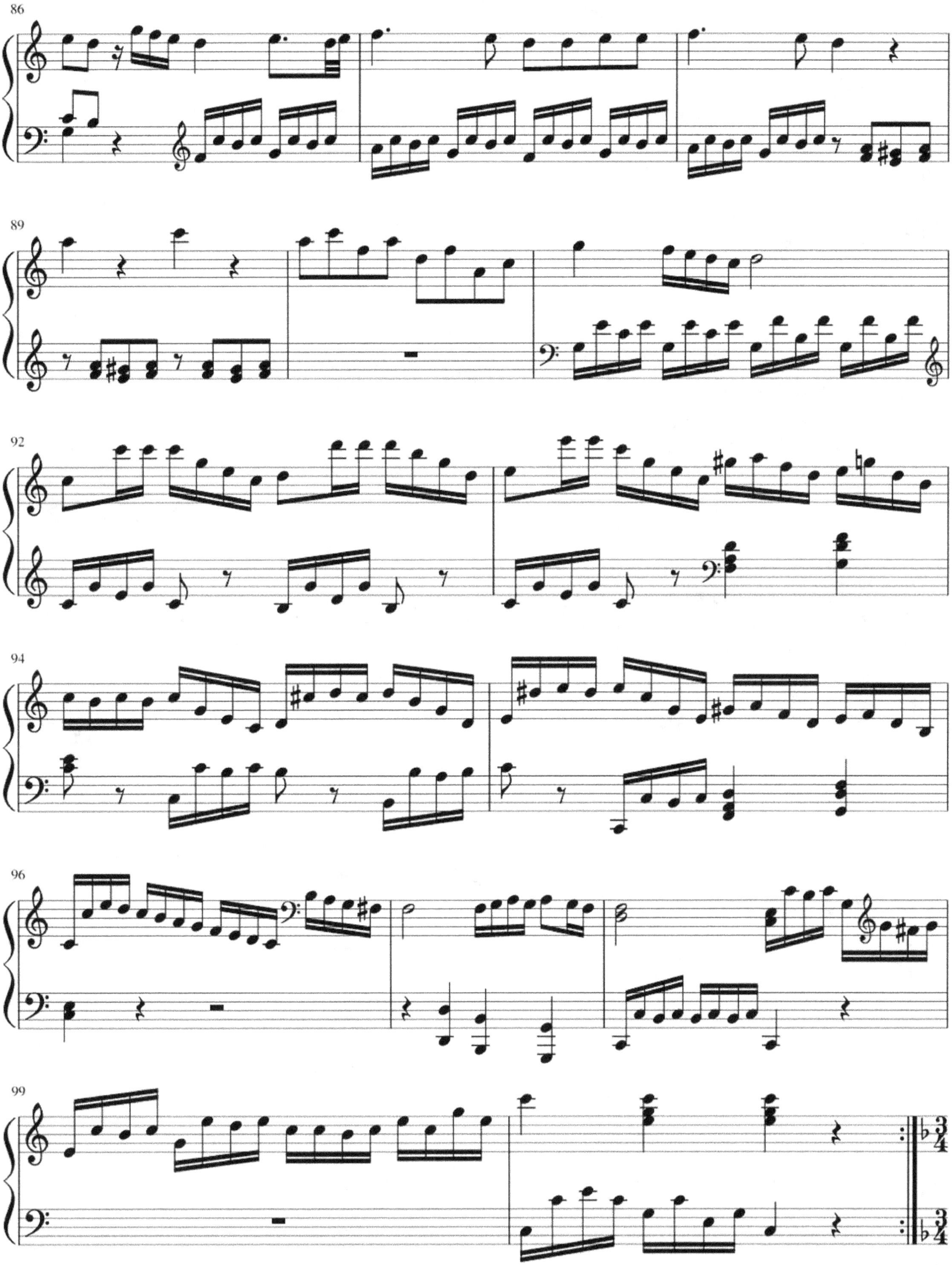
86
89
92
94
96
99

Sonata in C
K.279, 2nd Movement, Adante

Wolfgang Amadeus Mozart

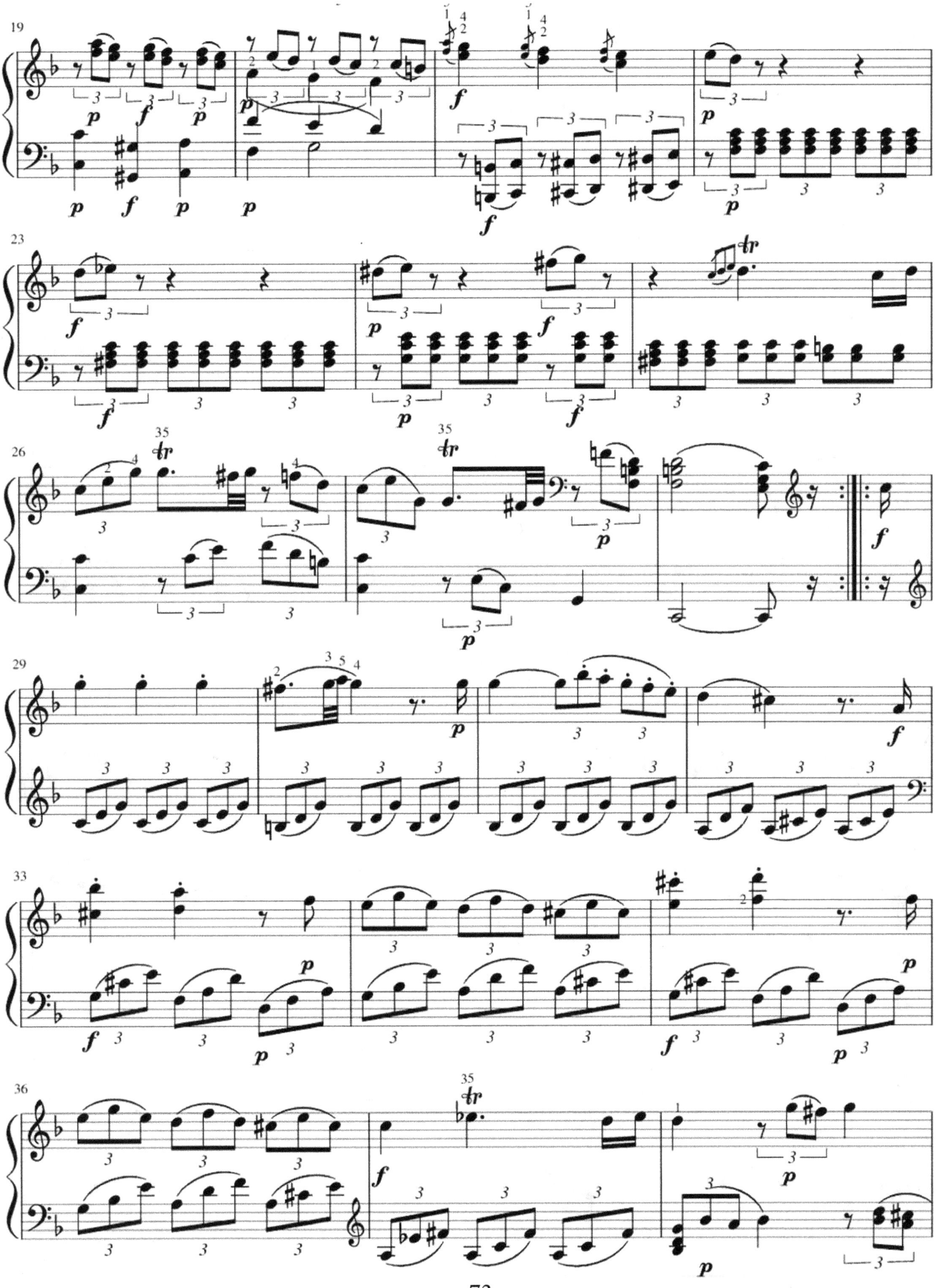
19
23
26
29
33
36

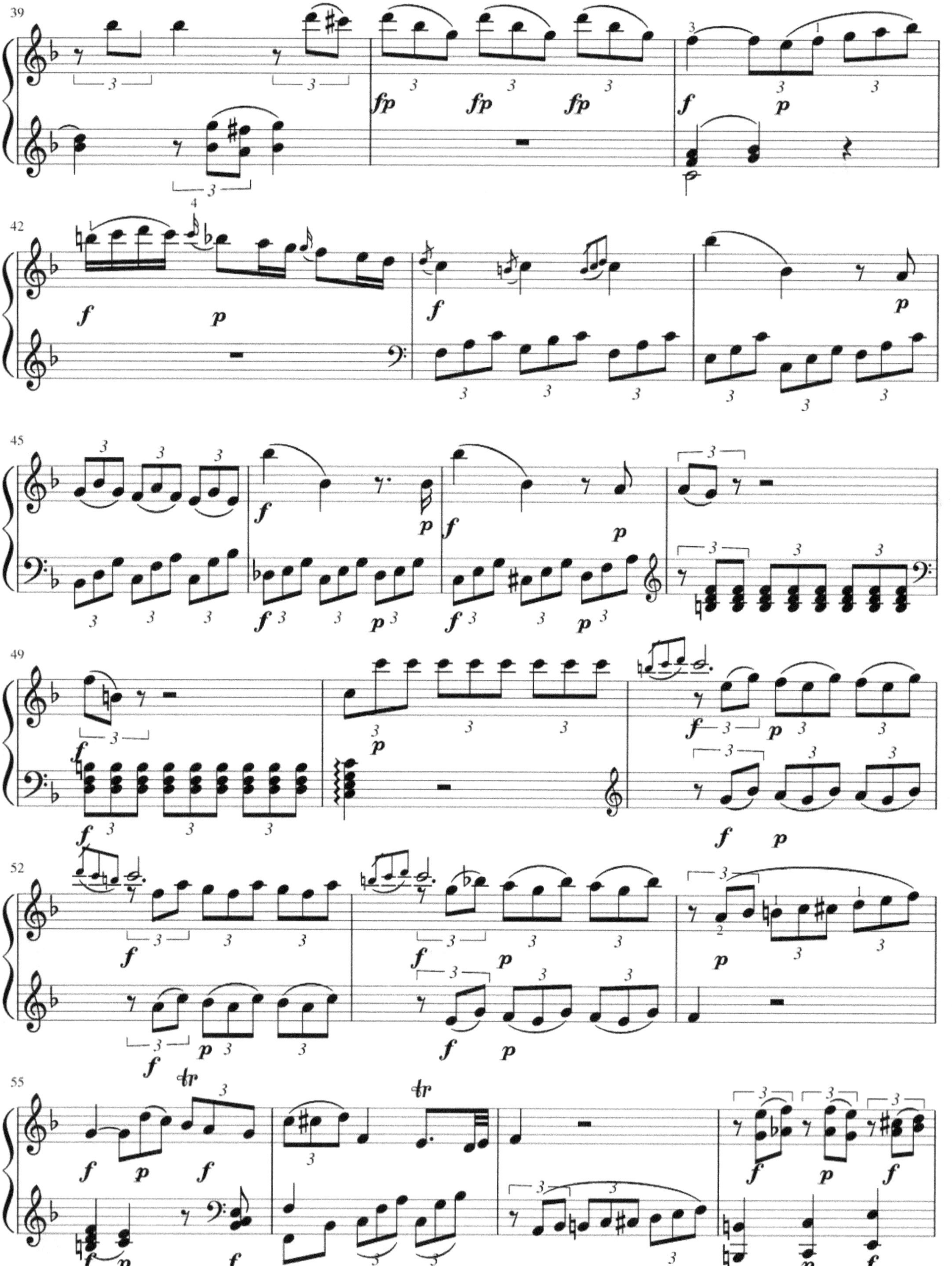
39
42
45
49
52
55

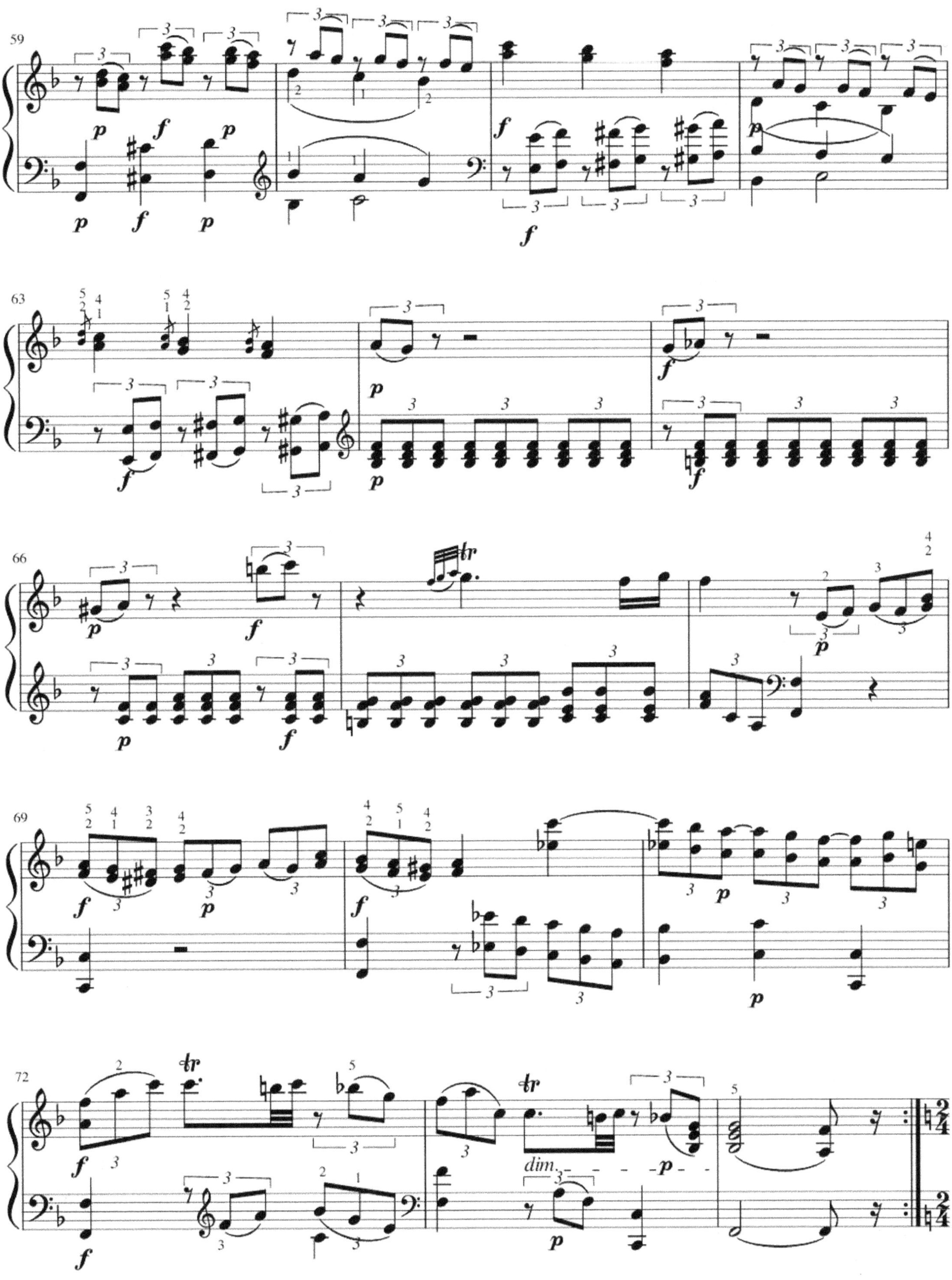
59
63
66
69
72
tr
dim.
p
f